RONALD SEARLE
IN PERSPECTIVE

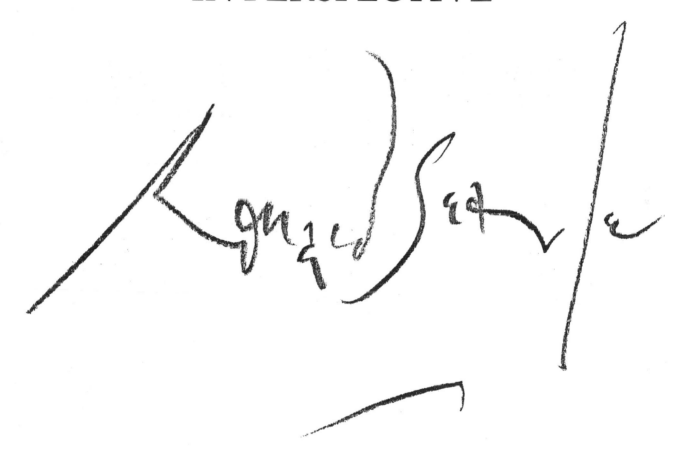

THE ATLANTIC MONTHLY PRESS

BOSTON • NEW YORK

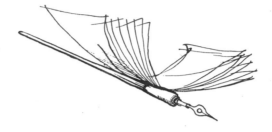

First American Edition

Library of Congress Cataloging in Publication Data

Searle, Ronald, 1920–
  Ronald Searle in perspective.

  1. English wit and humor, Pictorial. I. Title.
NC1479.S39A4   1985   741.6′092′4   84–48443
ISBN 0–87113–003–3

Printed in Great Britain

CONTENTS

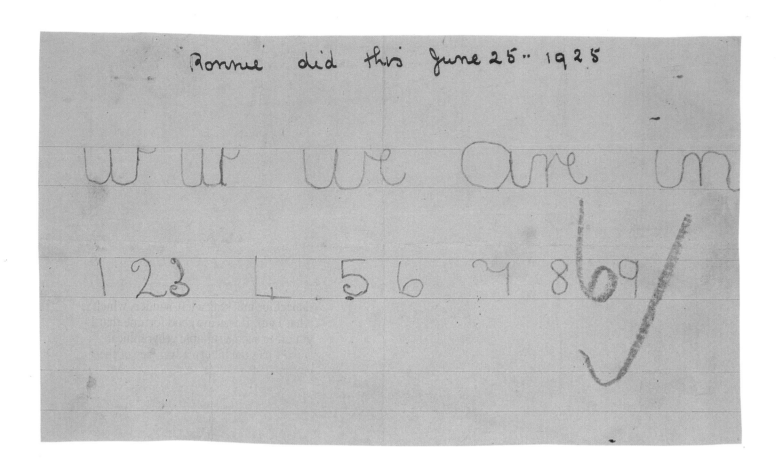

'Ronnie did this...'

On Sunday afternoons in Cambridge, during the late 'twenties, my father would walk me and my baby sister up the bleak Newmarket Road in which I was born, past the gas-works to Garlic Row, to visit his round and jolly sister, Beattie. Aunt Beat was married to a gloomy, thickset, silent man called Johnny Alsop, a milkman. Their house beside the family dairy was a postwar semi' and its glossy painted door was glorified by a rising sun with tastefully bevelled wooden rays, on a sky of dappled non-see-through glass.

There were occasions when we would arrive in front of this ever-rising sun, to find that Auntie Beat was still not back from visiting Uncle Sid, housepainter all week and fruitscape painter on Sunday, who lived further up in Coldham's Lane. However, her absence presented no problems to us because, as always, whenever Auntie Beat left the house she would carefully lock the front door, hide the key under the mat and hang a note on the letter-box saying: 'Key under mat'.

In a town like Cambridge, historically renowned for its eccentrics, the Searles were merely like the rest of the people of East Anglia. As the Auvergnats are regarded by the rest of the French as being a bit bizarre despite their cleverness in monopolising the *bois et charbons* bars of Paris, the other English looked askance at the somewhat special character of those who, like us, emerged from the bogs and swamps. Also, the fact that anyone would choose to remain in the insalubrious East Anglian climate for untold generations, was sufficient justification for considering the natives to be not only warped, but thick in the head.

As I said, our family was not particularly noticeable among these special people, despite the fact that my father's eldest sister, Edie, was known to dust the coal. There was, however, a slightly exotic difference in that his cousins Doddy and Joan were, at this time, earning their living on the music-hall stage as lady serpents. In brief costumes of fringed scales, Doddy and Joan would ooze about the stage of any theatre that had the courage to book them, hoping to be mistaken for wasp-waisted pythons.

always, he would be wearing an ancient 'deer-stalker', a voluminous raglan over his skinny, bowed body and, quite unconcernedly, an eighteen-inch coil of copper wire weighing at least fifteen pounds, round his neck. At the time no one considered this unusual, there was still room for everybody...

Quite suddenly I began to draw. I had been scribbling for ever. Now it took shape and I became, first fascinated, then obsessed, with what it was possible to do with pen and pencil. No one paid much attention to this, nor to the fact that the drawings were immediately grotesque. This was assumed to be one of the penalties for being 'cack-handed', local dialect for mocking a left-hander, which is what I am. It was my good fortune that I got off to such a suitable geographical start. I had the inborn advantage of the eccentric, the abnormal seeming to me, as well as to most of those around me, perfectly normal and not at all a caricature of 'proper' behaviour as demanded by 'them' from outside. In addition, nobody suggested that there was anything ludicrous in the fact that, for the first time since the Searles had plodded their way through the bogs to escape the Vikings, a left-handed Searle was proclaiming that he had to be An Artist, instead of a gravedigger, or whatever.

[*Above*] First pastels: *Mother* [1929]

The little faded hall of my grandmother's house was almost aggressively cluttered with framed sepia postcards of the girls' highly original but lowly billed act which, like so many other endearingly eccentric English music-hall turns, was to be driven into oblivion with the arrival of the American talking cinema. At least that was my grandma's theory and she stuck to it; refusing to see a 'talkie' until the day she died.

When I was old enough to be sent off to choir practice, I would frequently have to edge past old Professor J.J. Thompson, godfather of The Bomb. He would be spending his regular hour gazing absent-mindedly into the long established ladies' corset shop, next to the choirboys' entrance of St. Andrew the Great church – pondering, perhaps, an original method of harnessing the atom. On the way home again I would usually be greeted in Emmanuel Road by Mr. King, a friend of my father's and a renowned incunabulist, with the regal and timeless features of an Egyptian mummy, who would be striding along with the aid of a seven-foot staff. As

[*Below*] First paintbrush: *Design for a linocut* [1928]

Just as many East Anglians secreted toenail parings, stuck pins into wax dolls and drank far too much poppy tea, others loaded their pockets with an assortment of charms and went to wild lengths to appease superstition. Until I was in my teens, I never moved without a dried rabbit's foot, a piece of coal and a sprinkling of salt knotted in my breast-pocket handkerchief. Nothing abnormal, everyone was aware that everybody did it – at least among the families we knew – in the town and from the surrounding farming villages. My mother 'read' the fortunes of friends (and herself) in tea leaves, when they stopped by with eggs, or a gang of chitterlings, on their way to the Saturday market. She also had a rather scratched, black-painted, tin hatbox, in which she secreted bits of paper marking notable events. Among these, it now appears, was a curious slip bearing the garbled message: ' W W We are in 123 4 56 7 8 9 ', on which she had noted: 'Ronnie did this June 25th 1925'.

Whatever the hidden significance of this magic message, the charm seems to have done its stuff. Ronnie went on doing his thing relentlessly, egotistically, single-mindedly, obsessively and without a break, for a further (up to the time of writing) fifty-nine years.

As will have been noticed, W W We are in the slightly uncomfortable position of having been asked to introduce this exotic collection of pictures ourselves, instead of leaning conveniently on a German Professor of Fine Arts, or Groucho Marx, or some other kindly notable, as has happened in the past. True, we have the unique advantage of having known Searle better than anyone else for sixty-four years (come March) and, in addition have personally supervised this retrospective view which neatly covers forty-five years of on-going scratching, all the way from Cambridge blue-bottomed life class models, to recent dirty spy-exchanging Berlin situations.

Actually the exercise is extremely salutary. Once one has overcome the horror of that long, backward look, one or two things become apparent. From the artist's point of view, however seemingly diverse the subject-matter, the *oeuvre* has positive coherence, startling originality and masterly authority of line. The pneumatic bottom of the art school nude on page 9, is intimately (if I may say so) linked to that of the drunken kangaroo on page 175, drawn half a century later. The conclusion to be drawn from all this must be left to the usual responsible authorities. Coming from me it would be indelicate, wouldn't it?

RONALD SEARLE
March 1984

"I'm not sure, I think it is Tchaikovsky." [1939]

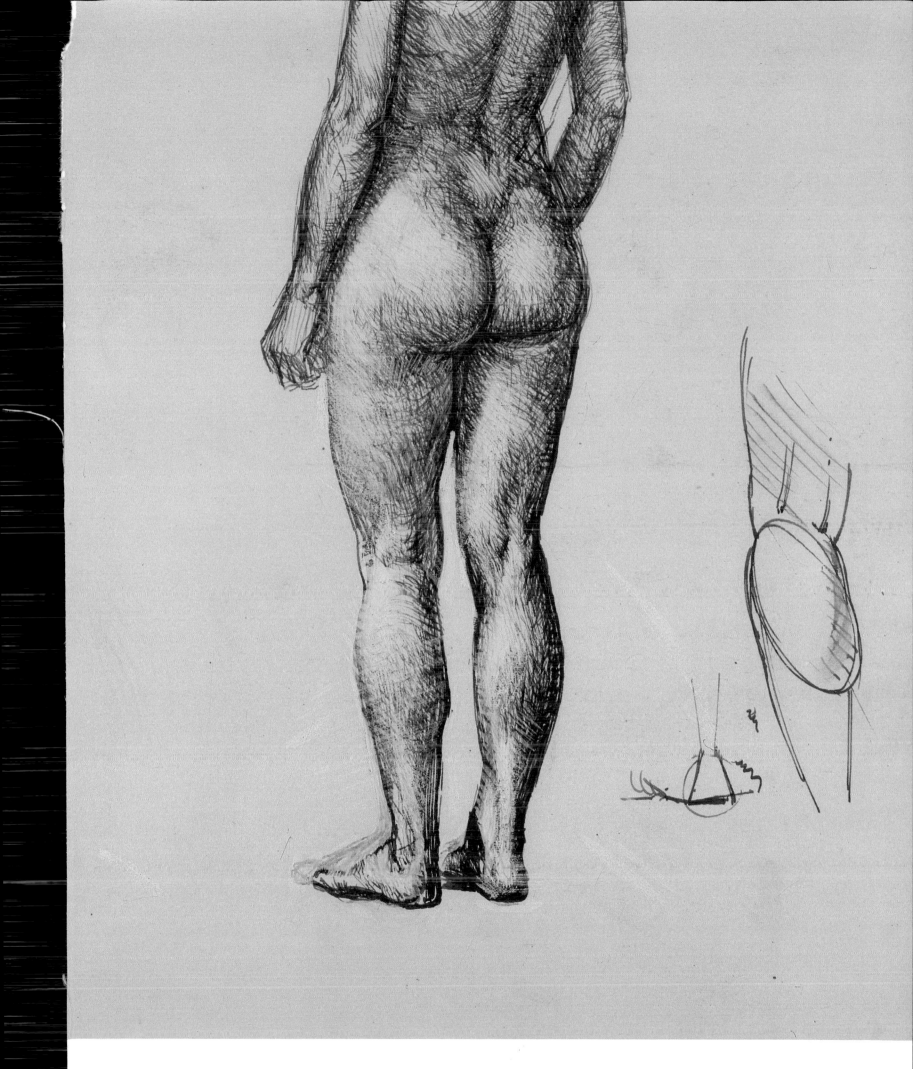

1938 – 1945 ART SCHOOL, ARMY & WAR

CAMBRIDGE SCHOOL OF ART

[*Above*] Very reclining model

[*Right*] A standing one

THE PHONEY WAR

Night Manoeuvres [1941]

Regulation haircut [1940]

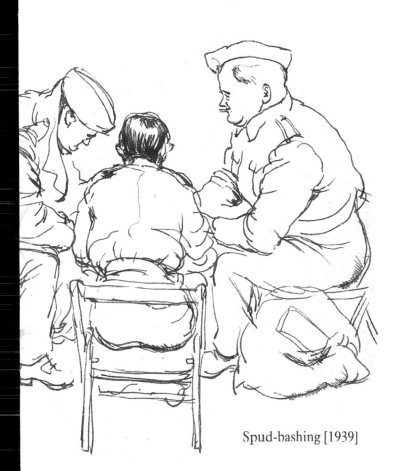

Spud-bashing [1939]

13

THE REAL THING...

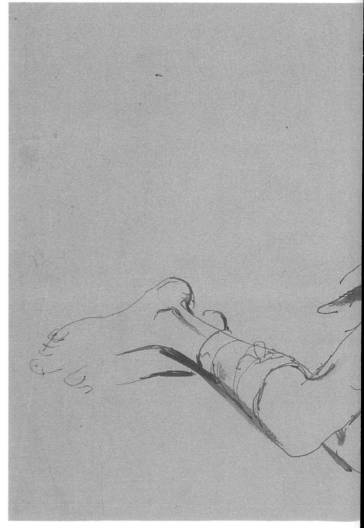

Ronald
Searle
Singapore 1944
—
Jap
Gestapo

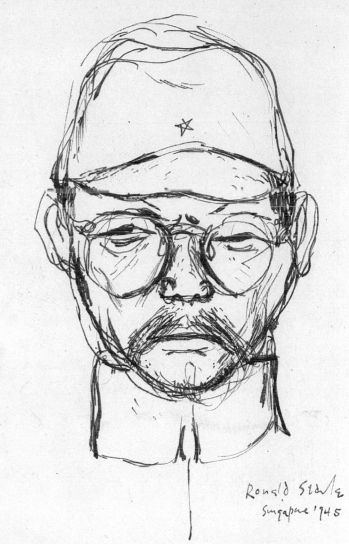

Ronald Searle
Singapore 1945

Ronald Searle. Singapore 1944

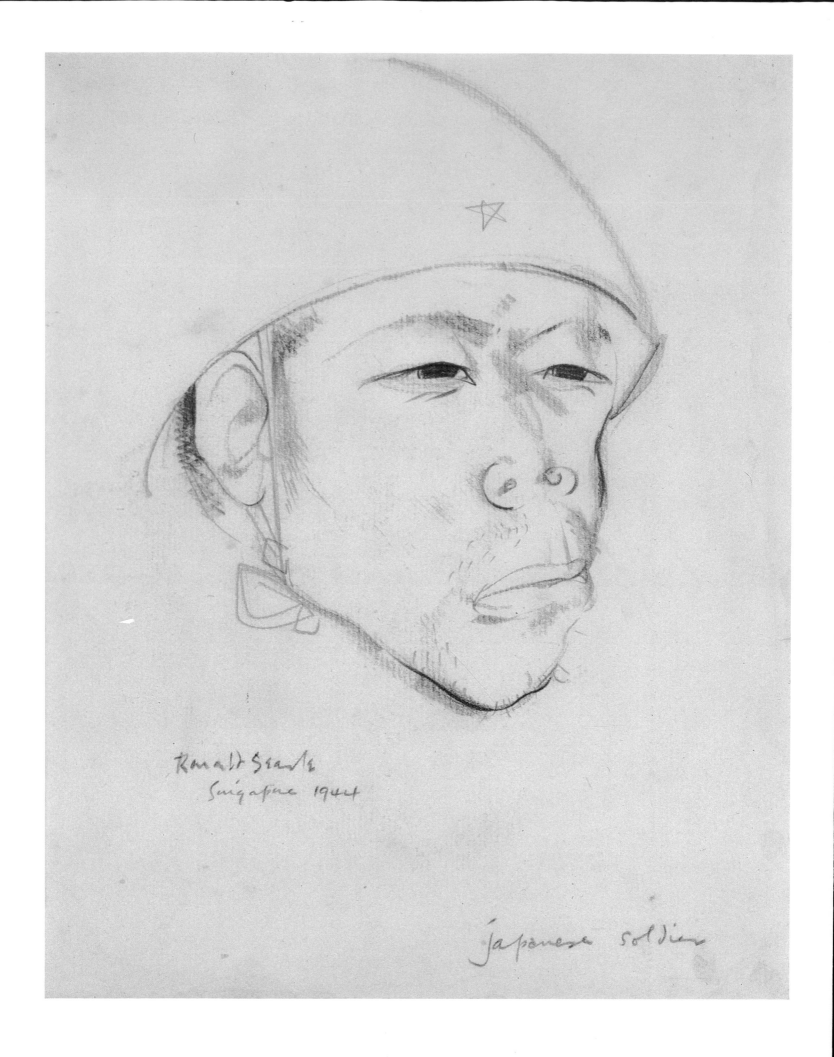

Guard [1944]

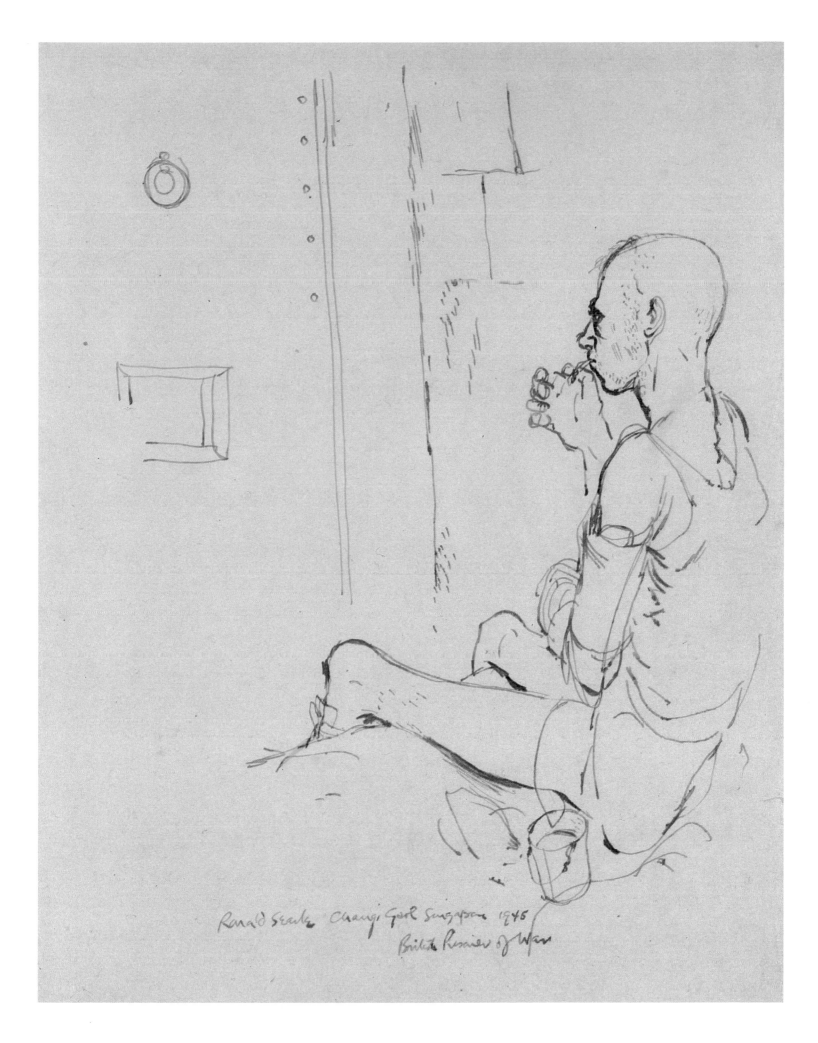

Prisoner [1945]

Christmas
Dinner 1944

Kensington Bus Stop, Winter 1947

At the Theatre: *The Stalls [1946]*

At the Theatre: "*So sorry…*" *[1946]*

Ronald Searle

Vranduk, Yugoslavia
Aug 22 1947

The Ruins of Warsaw

POLAND 1948

Ronald Searle

Brzyszkis Cathedral Krakow
Aug 15 1948

Street Scene, Kensington [1946]

"Some little girl didn't hear me say 'unarmed combat'."

"I didn't realise it took so long."

"Go on, say it – 'I promise to leave my body to Science'."

"I'll just die and then you'll be sorry."

"*Bloody sportsdays...*"

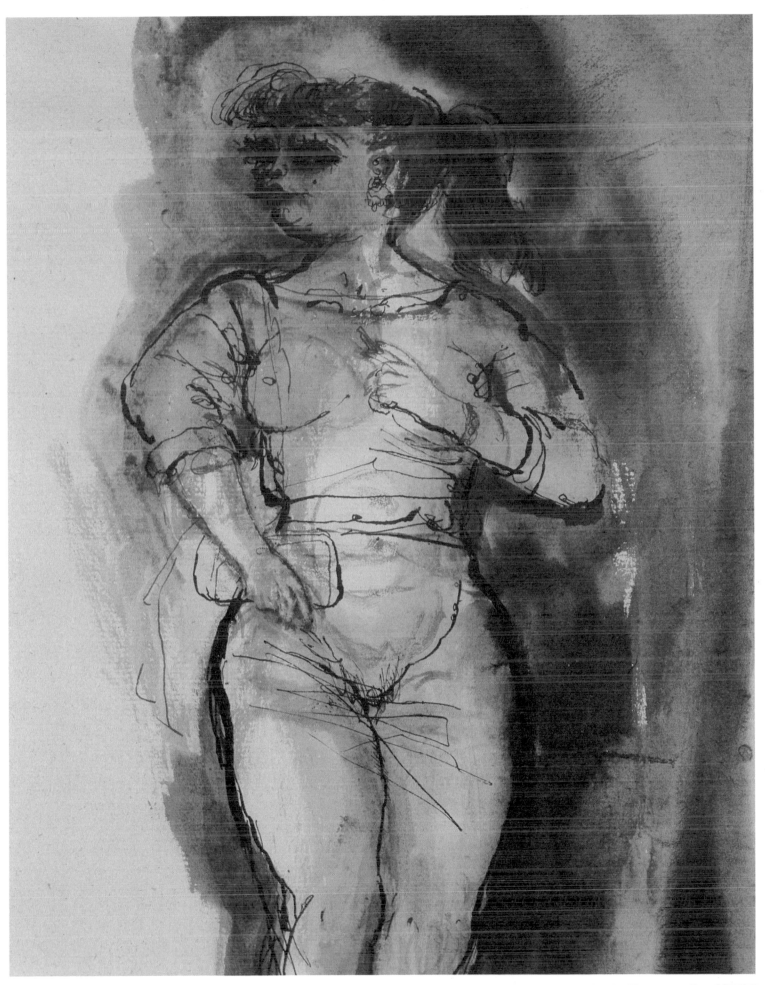

On the Bayswater Road [1950]

Street musician, London

Street Musicians, Portobello Road [1951]

Street musicians

The Bowery

The old Savoy Dance Hall, Harlem

Cocktail Time

[*Above*] Camp Laschenskyhof, near Salzburg

[*Below*] New Arrival, San Sabba Transit Camp, Trieste

REFUGEES 1959

Notes from a journey made for the
United Nations High Commissioner
for Refugees

Aversa Refugee Camp, near Naples

[*Above*] Police Quarantine, San Sabba Transit Camp, Trieste

[*Below*] Single Men's Dormitory, Camp Karls Kaserne, Vienna

"Of course, you're lucky – yours curls naturally." (1956)

Majesty of the Law [1959]

House of Commons, 1955: *Churchill's last speech*

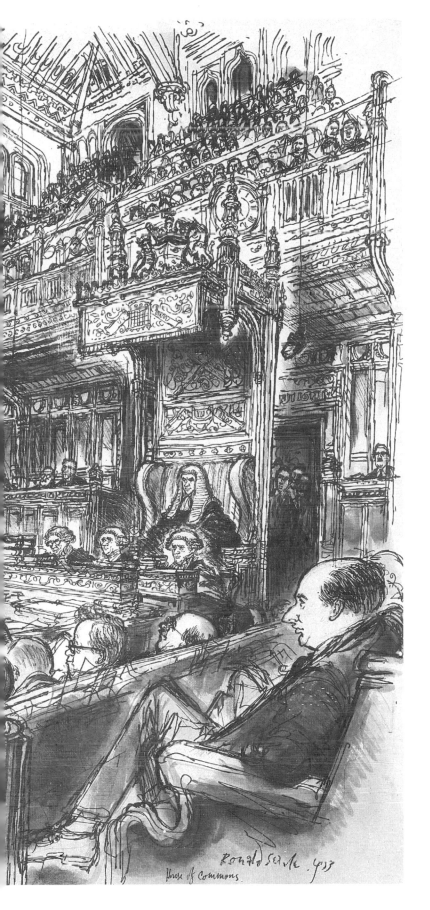

House of Commons

Paris, 1958

Nixonites

On the road with Kennedy

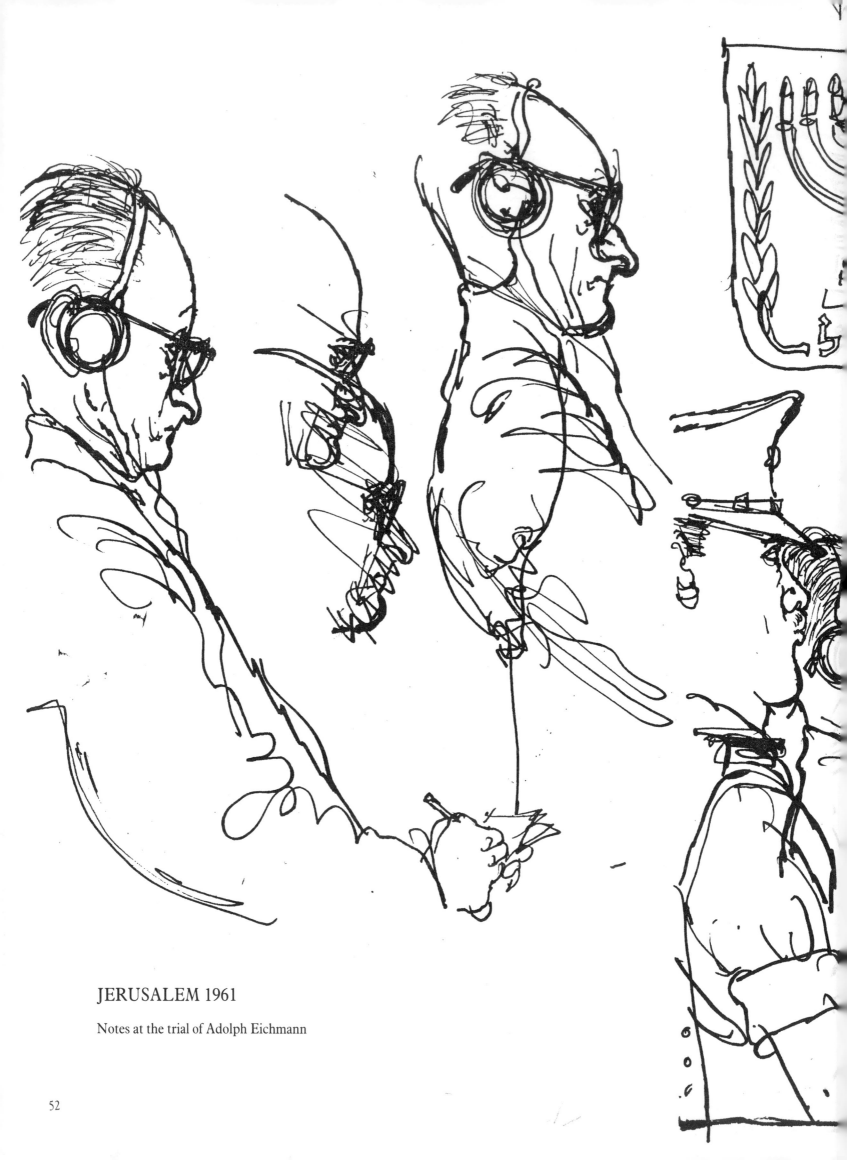

JERUSALEM 1961

Notes at the trial of Adolph Eichmann

53

Russia for Beginners (1960)

UKRAINE: Secret Soviet Missile Base

TAKE ONE TOAD...

From a book of Ancient Remedies

DEATH and suchlike afflictions of some severity

For not allowing death to come and fetch a man:
Recite the names of the gods seven times each over
all their drawings, and hang the drawings around
the neck of the man for whose benefit the charm
was made. He will be protected from all
misfortune.

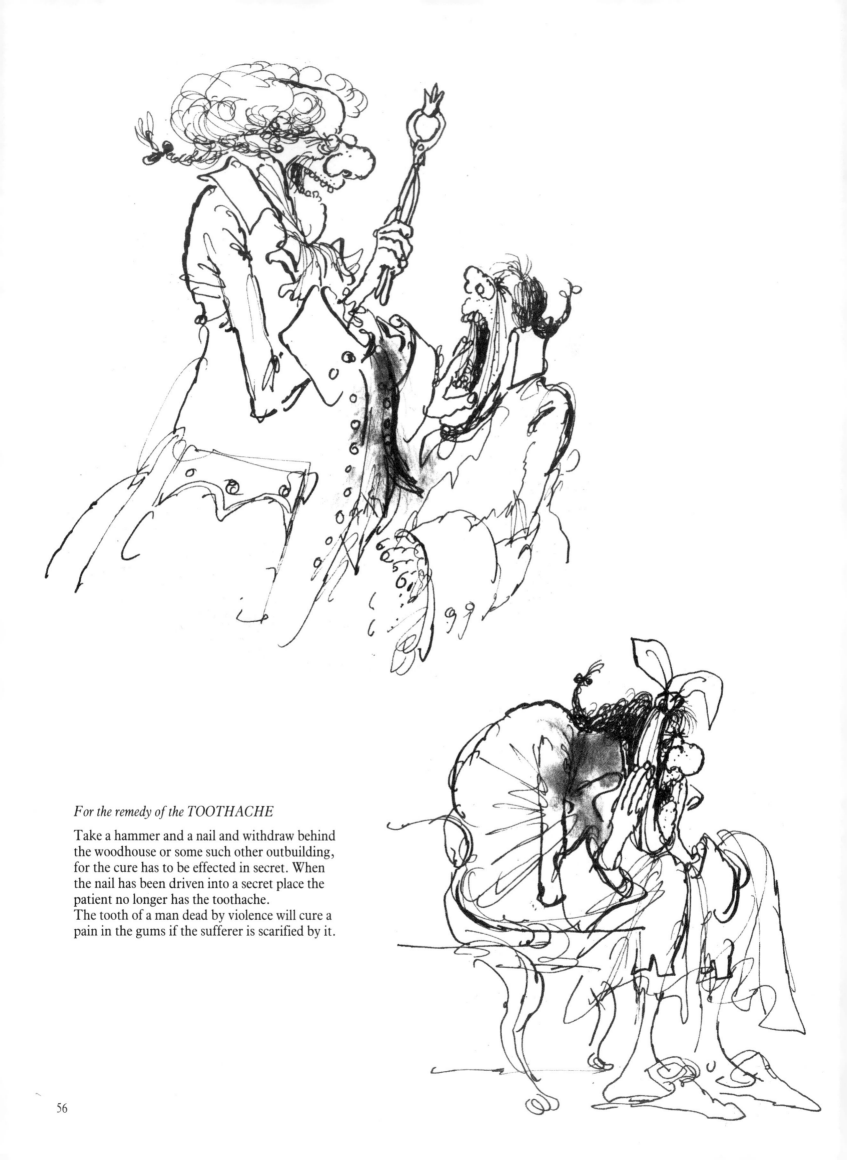

For the remedy of the TOOTHACHE

Take a hammer and a nail and withdraw behind
the woodhouse or some such other outbuilding,
for the cure has to be effected in secret. When
the nail has been driven into a secret place the
patient no longer has the toothache.
The tooth of a man dead by violence will cure a
pain in the gums if the sufferer is scarified by it.

For the treatment of ULCERS, CANCERS, TUMOURS and MALIGNANCIES of an irritating nature.

Persons suffering from ulcerous affections of the mouth – thrush – may be cured by having a person born posthumously blow into their mouth.
The laying on of the hand of a corpse is said to give temporary relief.

MALIGNANT SORE THROAT

Take a small frog and, holding it by the hind
legs, retain it in the mouth for several minutes.
During this time it will suck out the poison, and
the patient will recover.

[1968]

[1966]

The Second Coming of Toulouse-Lautrec [1969]

The Second Coming of Toulouse-Lautrec:
The Labours of Hercules [1969]

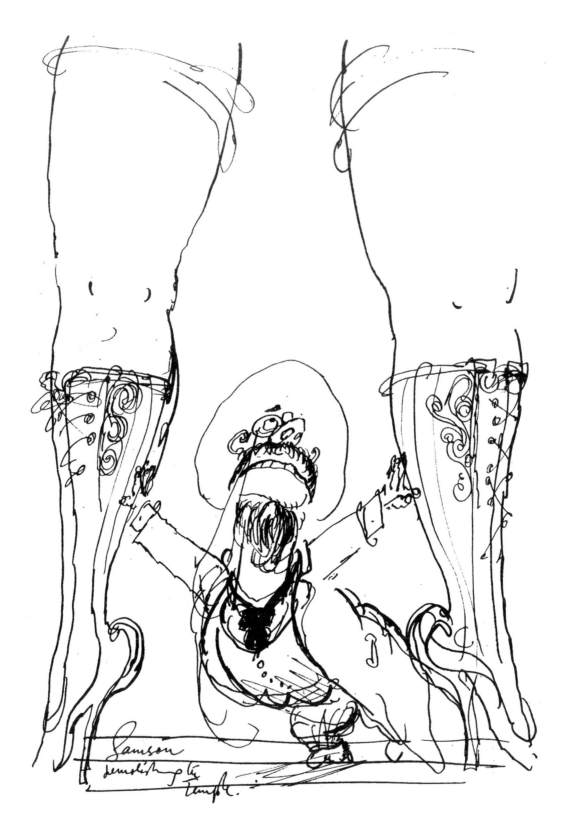

Samson Demolishing the Temple [1969]

Those Magnificent Men in Their
Flying Machines, a film [1965]

CAMBRIDGE 1964: *"Granta" Reveals All*

Cover for a student magazine

LONDON 1961: *"Are you sure this is Chris Barber's place?"*

EAST BERLIN [1964]

BLACK FOREST [1963]

PALM SPRINGS, California [1963]

Baseball, Phoenix, Arizona [1963]

Hudson's Bay Post, Maliotenam, Canada [1963]

CASABLANCA [1965]

74

Sunset, Oahu [1965]

Ronald Searle Oahu '65

Hamburg St. Pauli [1967]

[1967]

Papa Doc', Haiti [1968]

The Wall, Berlin [1963]

[1972]

The Outsider [1977]

[1976]

Déjeuner sur
l'herbe [1976]

Pigs [1974]

Ronald Searle

Slick

The New York Times

People [1978]

Horsepower

Horsepower [1979]

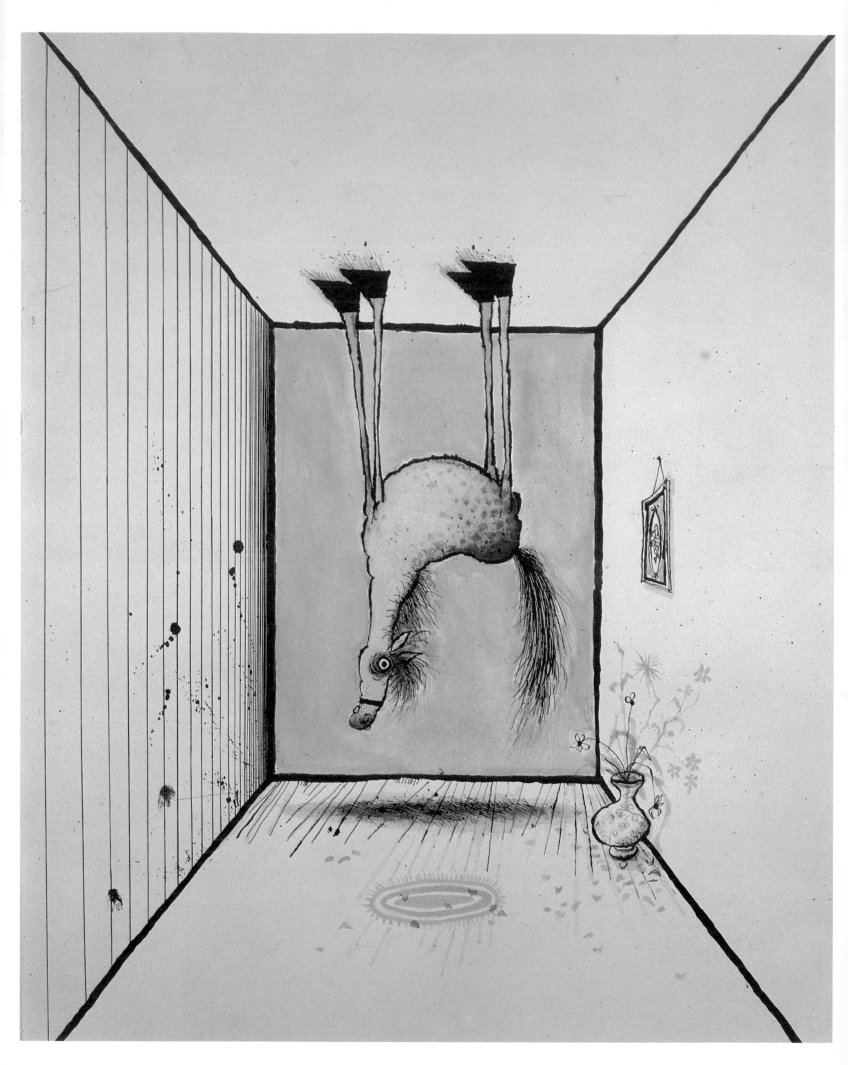

Pegasus Returns [1972]

[1979]

[1976]

Emergence of MS-tique USA [1973], with
a nod to Hogarth's *Rake's Progress* [1733]

DEBUT

Bursts upon the social scene in
a madcap whirl of men and money.

SUCCESS

Popular with college classmates,
pursues studies in natural history.

DISILLUSIONMENT

Marries conglomerateur, bewails
subsidiary status.

TEMPTATION

Becomes radical feminist,
storms male bastions.

DEGRADATION

Emerges as national spokesperson
for the movement.

DOWNFALL

Testifies before Senate committee
on Subversive Sexuality.

RUIN

Appointed to U.S. Cabinet, first
of her gender to become Secretary
of Defense.

[1979]

Secretary to the Big Boys [1974]

Bureaucrat [1974]

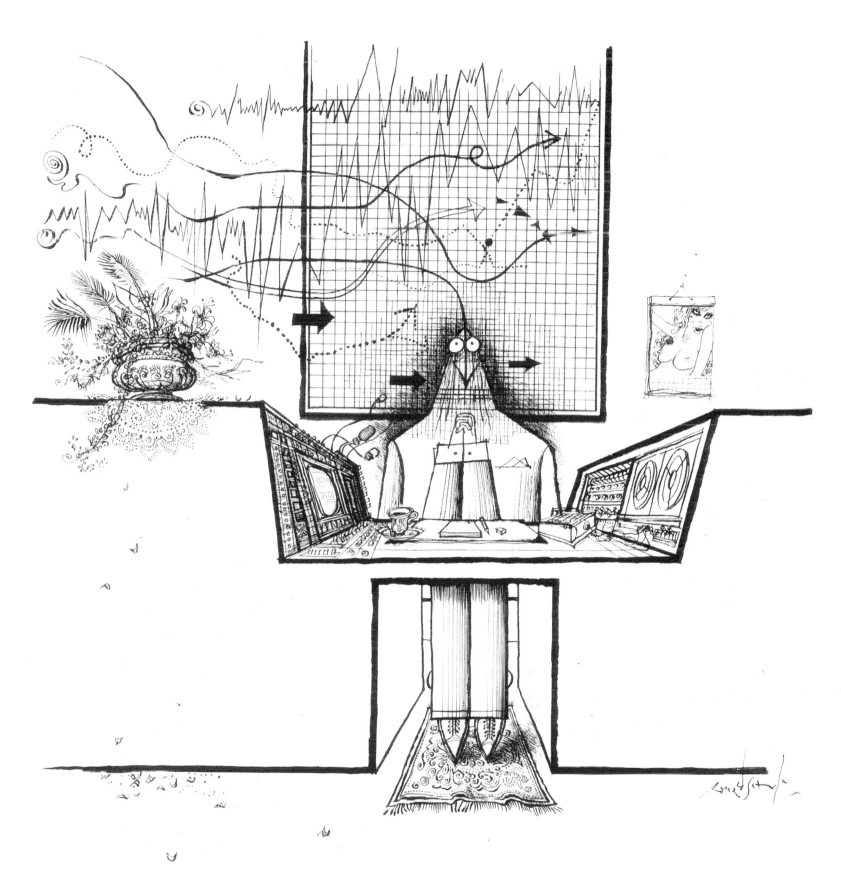

Technocrat [1974]

Hire and Fire [1974]

Workaholic [1974]

Upper Reaches [1974]

Spokesperson [1974]

The Manger [1974]

MONEY: The Speculator [1973]

MONEY: Means nothing to me [1978]

MONEY: Hello! Big Timer [1972]

Racin' [1979]

THE KILL

Huntin' [1978]

Swingin' [1974]

Thinkin' [1979]

[1972]

SOME SIGNS OF THE

Zoodiac

[1977]

LEO

SCORPIO

LIBRA

VIRGO

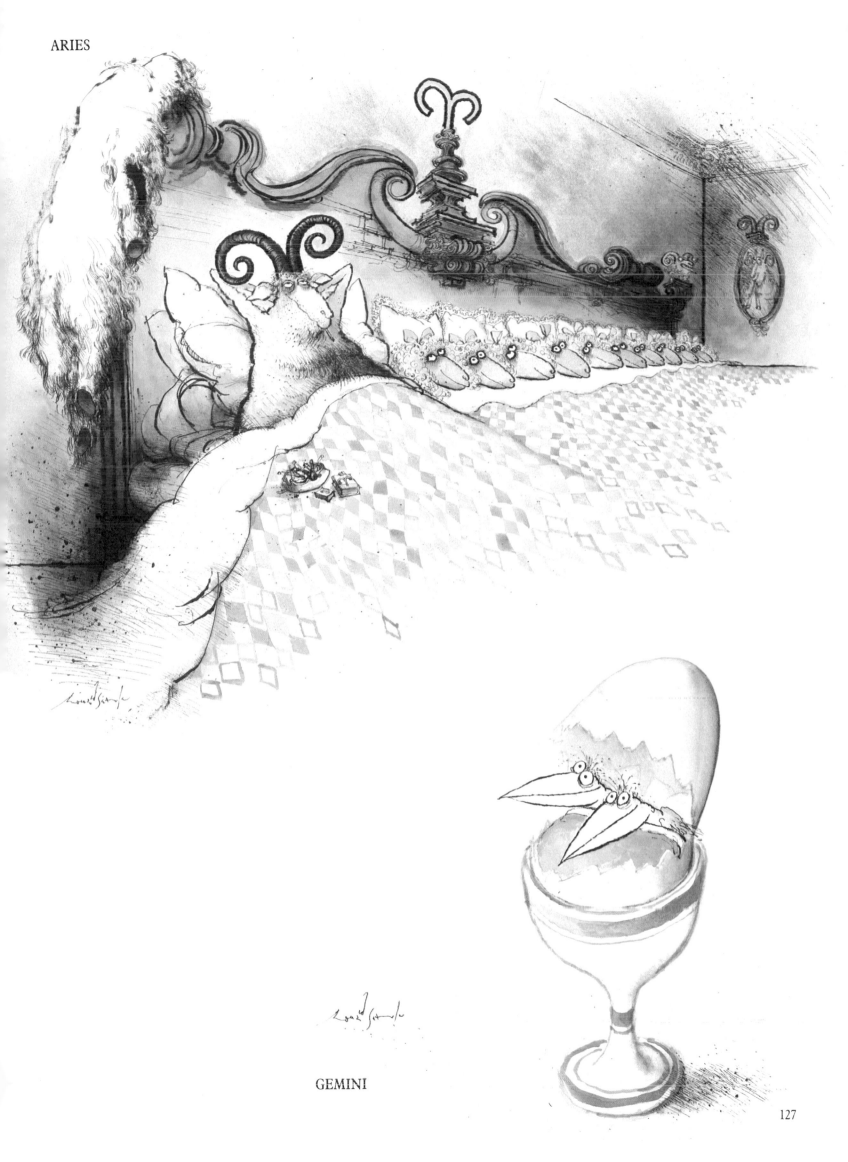

GEMINI

[1979]

Pastoral [1975]

Mickey Monument [1971]

Bookjacket design (1972)

Haven't We Met Before Somewhere?

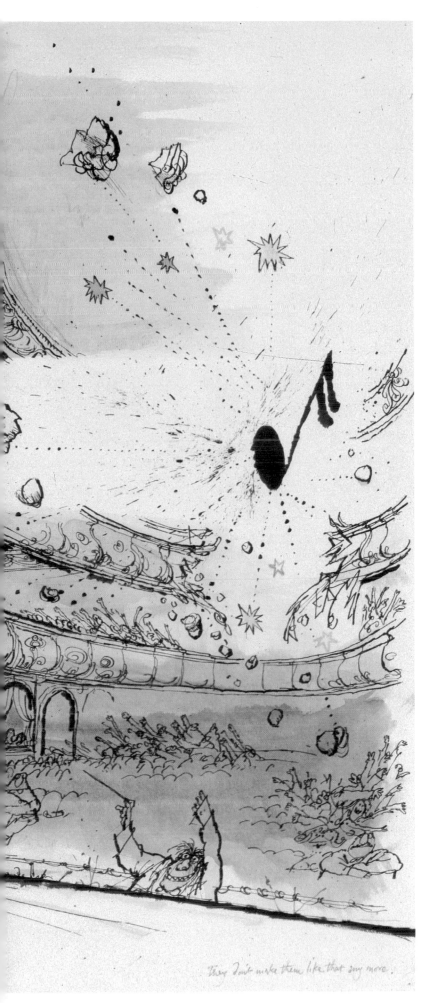

They Don't Make Them
Like That Anymore [1978]

The Kojak Connection [1975]

The Pickled Gudgeon Connection [1971]

Poster for the Royal Choral Society, London (1972)

'God Bless You, Merry Gentlemen...'

For the Good of the People [1977]

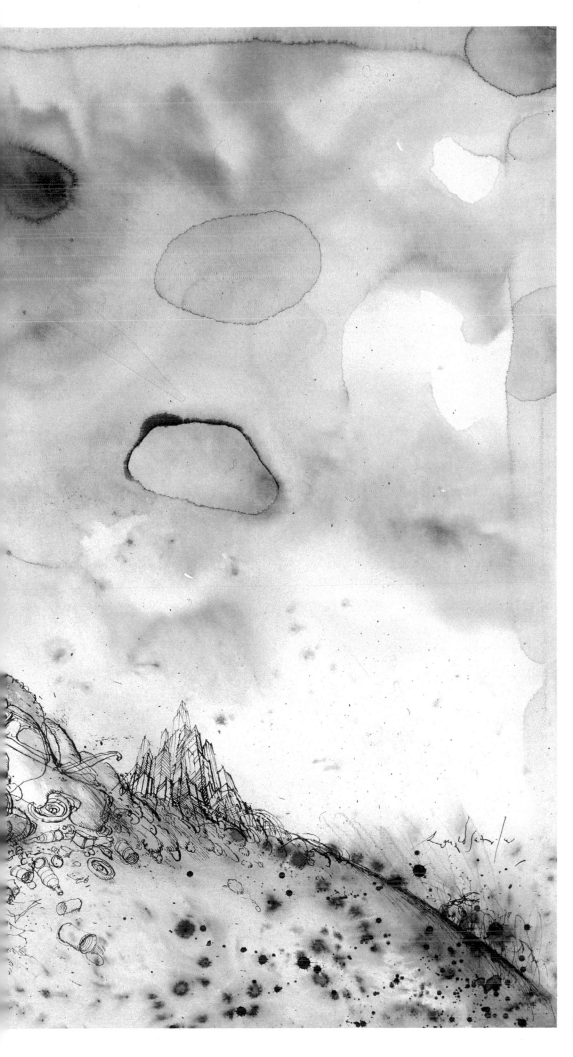

[1978]

For UNICEF Year of the Child [1979]

[1970]

The Last Customer [1973]

Sorceress [1978]

THE 'EIGHTIES

Study for the mislaid masterpiece
the Raft of the "Méduse"
by Toulouse-Lautrec.

[1980]

Some Mislaid Masterpieces

Mislaid Masterpieces:

MONA'S SISTER, GLADYS
by Leonardo Da Vinci
[1452-1519]

Mona [or Monna] Lisa Gherardini del Giocondo's younger and more cheerful sister, Gladys.

The portrait was painted about 1510, shortly before Gladys set off for Rome, to seek her fortune – again.

Mislaid Masterpieces:

THE PEACEABLE KINGDOM
by Edward Hicks [1790-1849]
The first version, c. 1829

Hicks, a cynical Bucks County Quaker, painted this splendid satire on the prophesy of Isiah, to keep the wolf from his door. However, despite its originality and underlying masterly academic structure, it did not sell and was put aside. It was suggested to Hicks that he was being somewhat naîve for not cashing-in on the current American Primitive Art wave and, after a few months seclusion with a New York dealer, he acknowledged the error of his ways. The one hundred sloppy versions of the same subject, which followed between 1830 and 1840, have been proclaimed works of genius and in the mainstream of the flowering-of-American-folk-art situation.

[1974]

Mislaid Masterpieces:
SWINGER
by Jean-Honoré Fragonard
[1732-1806]

Despite its vivacity and virtuosity, this painting
[c. 1765] was heavily criticised at the time, for not
being sufficiently vacuous. Furious, Fragonard
revised the subject as *L'Escarpolette*, [Wallace
Collection, London], in which he placed even more
emphasis on the bestial behaviour of the
participants.

Mislaid Masterpieces:

THE RAFT OF THE "MÉDUSE"
BY Henri de Toulouse-Lautrec
[1864 – 1901]

The existence of Toulouse-Lautrec's remarkable painting, is known from this photograph taken about 1895, by Maurice Guibert [as usual], in Lautrec's atelier at 27, rue Caulaincourt. Lautrec's interpretation should not be confused with that of Théodore Géricault [1791-1824], in the Louvre somewhere, which shows the sighting of the rescue ship *Argus*, by the few wretched survivors of the shipwrecked frigate *Méduse*, in 1816. On which occasion 149 souls were abandoned on a raft, with only casks of wine as nourishment.

Lautrec radically changes the emphasis by reducing the casks to bottles and the fifteen known survivors to eleven. Also, less anguishing than the version by Géricault and more in the spirit of his own times, the wrecking of Lautrec's *Méduse* has taken place on dry land.

157

Mislaid Masterpieces:

SWINE LAKE
[Later known as Pig Lake]

Ballet in four acts by Begitchev and Geltzer.
Music by P.I. Tchaikovsky

Owing to a misunderstanding by Julius Reisinger,
who thought he had heard Tchaikovsky asking him
to choreograph a ballet about swans, the first
production, at the Bolshoi Theatre, Moscow in
1877, opened as *Swan Lake*. Consequently *Swine
Lake* was put on ice for the time being and the title
revised to avoid further confusion.

In 1895, a choreography for *Pig Lake* was roughly
roughed out by Petipa, whilst waiting for the bus.
But he mislaid the dossier before the devoted
Ivanov could pull it together for the Maryinsky
company. Under the circumstances, they settled for
Swan Lake again – which was just as well, as the
backers were Arab.

Mislaid Masterpieces:
LES TRES PAUVRES HEURES DU DUC DE
BERRY [detail]
Ecole Française, XVe siècle

Mislaid Masterpieces:
SELF-PORTRAIT AS A NON-STOP SELF-
MUTILATOR by Vincent van Gogh [1853-1890]

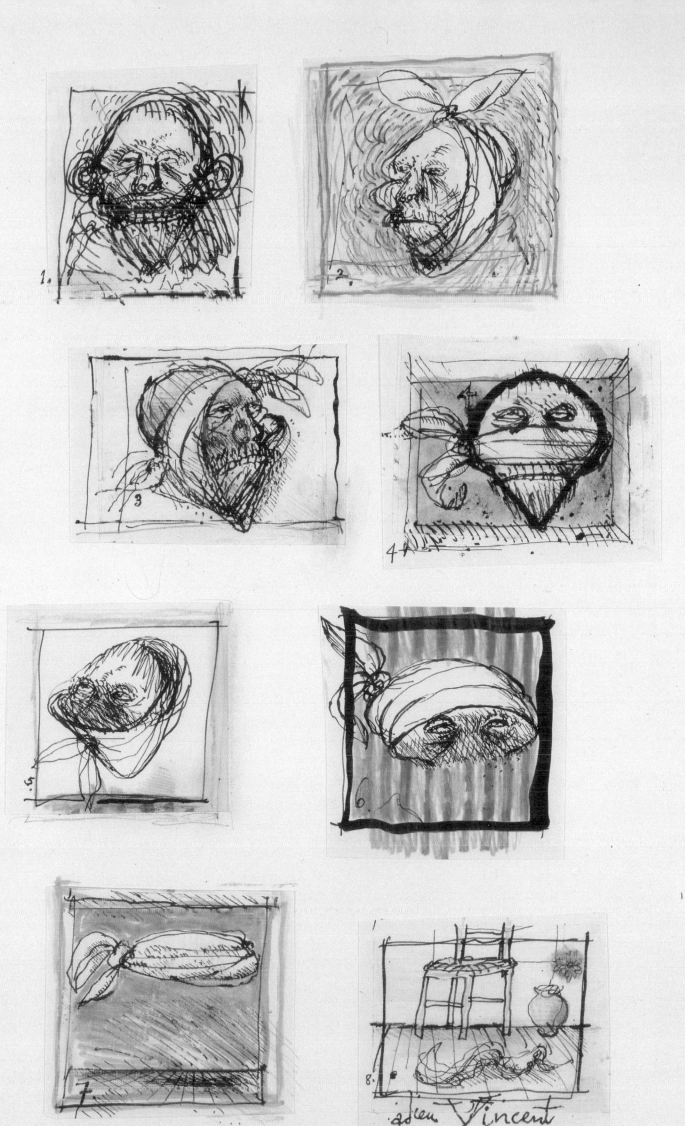

adieu Vincent

Mislaid Masterpieces:
BONJOUR MONSIEUR COURBET by Gustave
Courbet [1819-1877]
The first draft, c.1853

The Situation is Hopeless

Out-of-touch unicorn unaware that it is a myth

American bald eagle suddenly realising that
its leanings are basically Marxist

Hopelessly mixed-up vampire bat
trying to conceal the fact that its
tastes are rigidly vegetarian

Under-sexed double-horned rhinoccros
in search of a reliable aphrodisiac

Conceited egg about to commence its memoirs

Look – no animals. (An exercise.)

Annual Reunion of the Confrérie of Cork Sniffers

The Annual Non-Arrival of the English Grape Ceremony

AUSTRALIA: Uncorking the Kangarouge

GERMANY: The Ancient, Noble (and Secret) Ceremony
of Slashing the Trockenbeerenauslese

FRANCE: The Annual Festival of Welcome to Italian Wines

The Japanese Wine Ceremony

だす。女房のこわい兵隊は右へ出ろ。こわくないのは左へ出ろ。するとたちまち一〇〇人のうち九十九人の兵隊が右へ出た。左へ出たのは一人きりだった。隊長はその男のところへかけつけて、感動して、お前だけがほんとの人民英雄だと叫んで、肩をたたいた。するとその男は恐縮し、ひくいひくい声ではずかしそうに、いえ、ナニ、私、女房にいつも、みんなのあとについていってはいけないと、いわれつけてるもんですからと、答えた。

中国の民話には強妻や猛女がよく登場する。あの大陸ではどえらい大昔から伝統として一貫してオンナが強いらしい。女の帝王、女の海賊、女の革命家、女のテロリストなど、たどるどころにいくらでも指が折れる。気の強い女としては最近では江青女史の例があるけれど、彼女はその典型の一例であって、例外でも何でもない。今さらキモをつぶしたり、目玉パチクリしてはいけないのだ。これにつけるクスリは何もないから、せいぜい頭を低くして、負ケルガ勝、負ケルガ勝と呪文のように呟いておくことですナ。

ルーマニアの首都のブカレストで、ある夜、年配の国会議員と食事をしたことがあった。ぶどう酒がまわってそろそろおたがいに頬が夕焼色になったところを見はからってこの小話をやってみたら、議員氏、顎をそらせて哄笑する。そこで、もしあなたが兵隊であって隊長におなじ命令をだされたらどうします、右へ出ますか、左へ出ますかと、たずねてみた。すると議員氏はナプキンで口をぬぐいつつ、ごぞんじのようにわが国は社会主義国でありますから、大衆のあとについていくのが私の義務でありますと、答えた。

つぎにチェコの首都、プラーハ。通訳として私を毎日、案内してくれたのが女子大生で、アメリカ文学を専攻し、もっぱらノーマン・メイラーを読んでいるとのことだった。この女子大生と、ある夕方、どっしりと重い、すばらしいピルゼン・ビールを飲みつつ、この小話をし、ルーマニアの議員氏にしたのとおなじ質問をしてみた。あなたの夫ならどうするだろうかと。すると彼女は、夫のことは夫が考えるだろうから、私のことは私が考えるわと言下に答えた。

イラストレーション/ロナルド・サール

これは二十年前に中国へいったときに北京で宴会の席で聞かされた小話であるが、それ以後どこへいってもチャンスさえあれば流布でないとわからないけど、私が男なら一も二もなく右へいっちゃわネといって、大笑した。

God Yama and a Dead Soul
*Publicity for Suntory Old [Japanese] Whisky,
Tokyo [1981]*

The Encounter [1981]

Confused Albatross shooting an Ancient Mariner

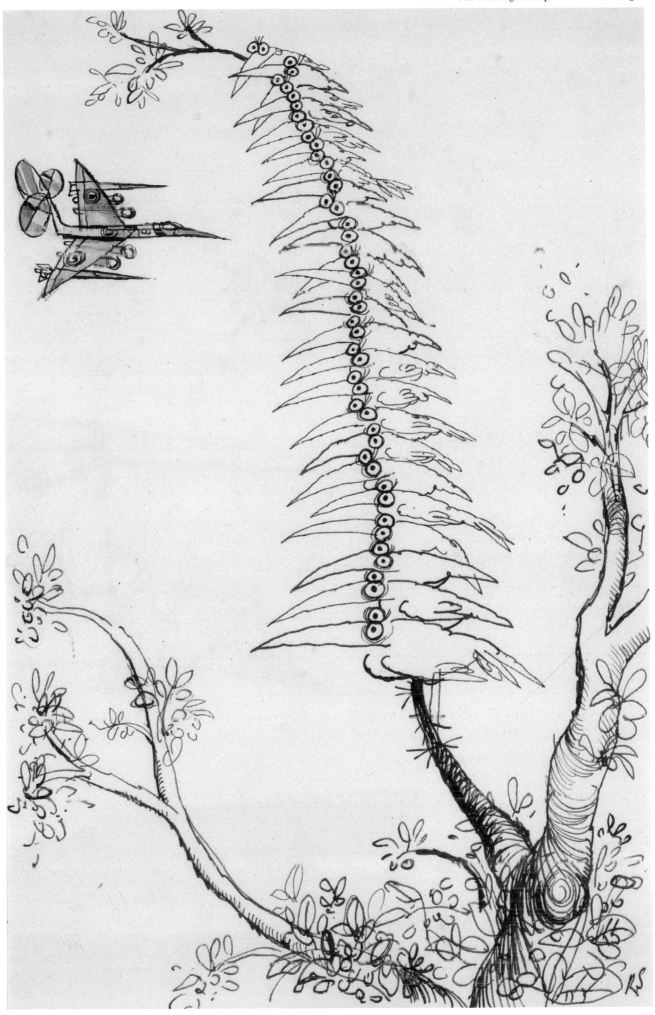

Strictly for the Birds

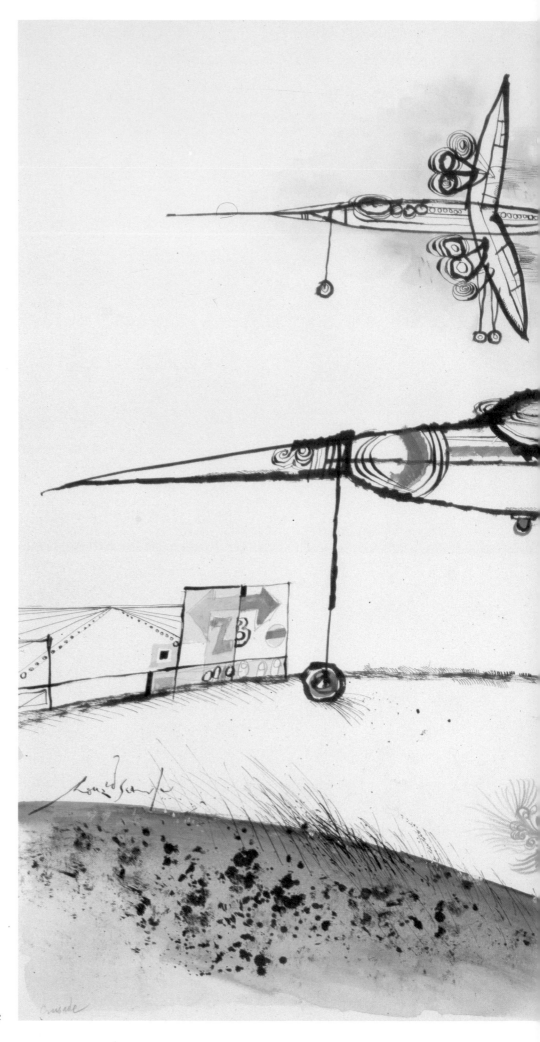

Crusade

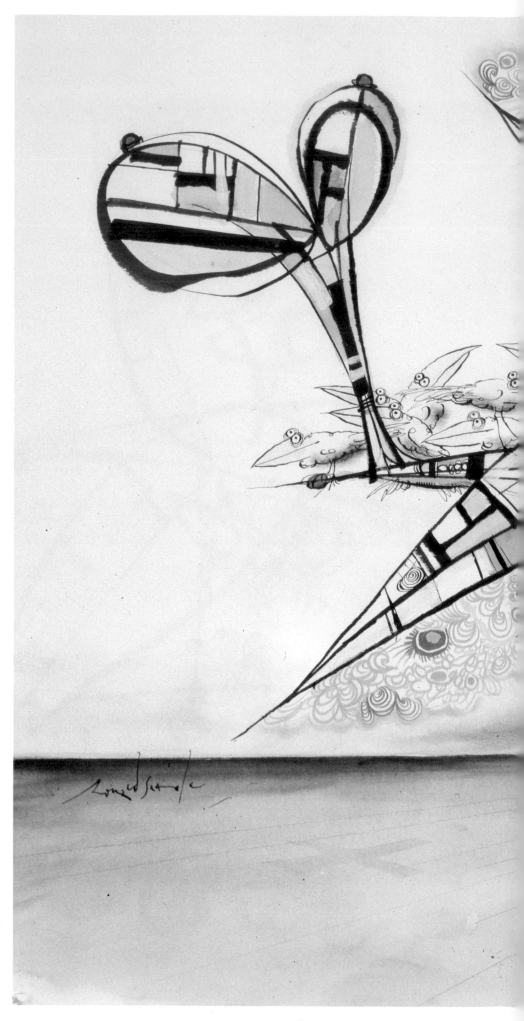

Warm Engines

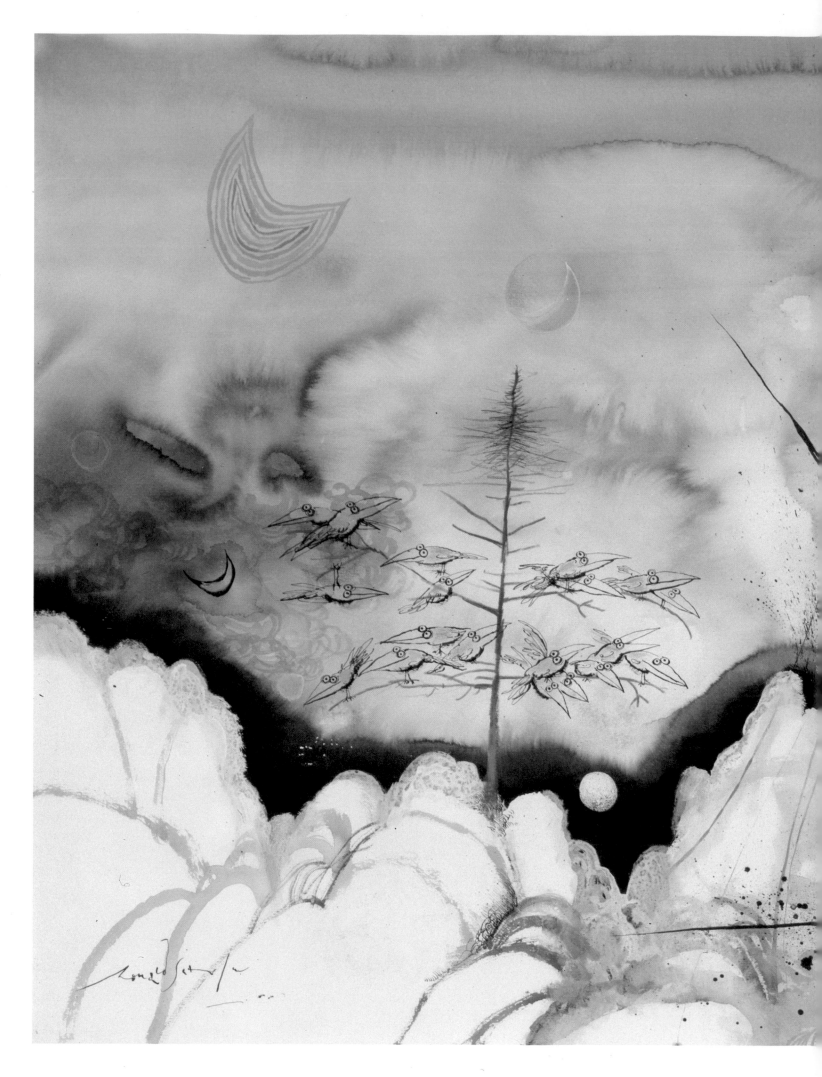

Wake

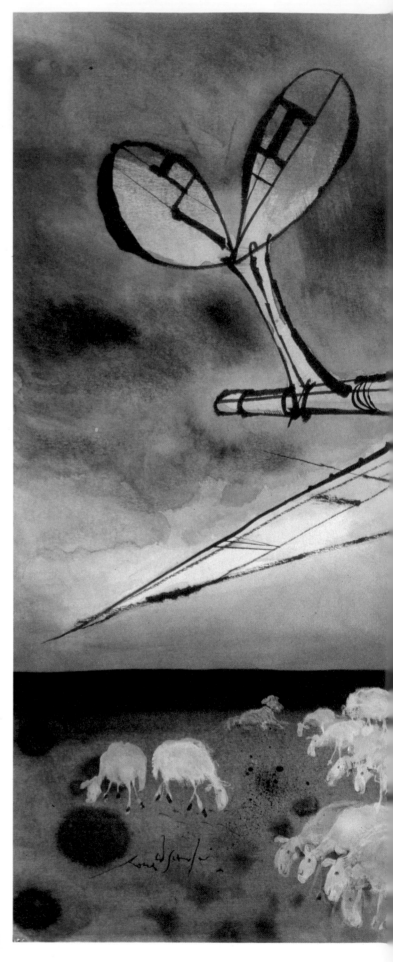

Irresistible force meets immovable object

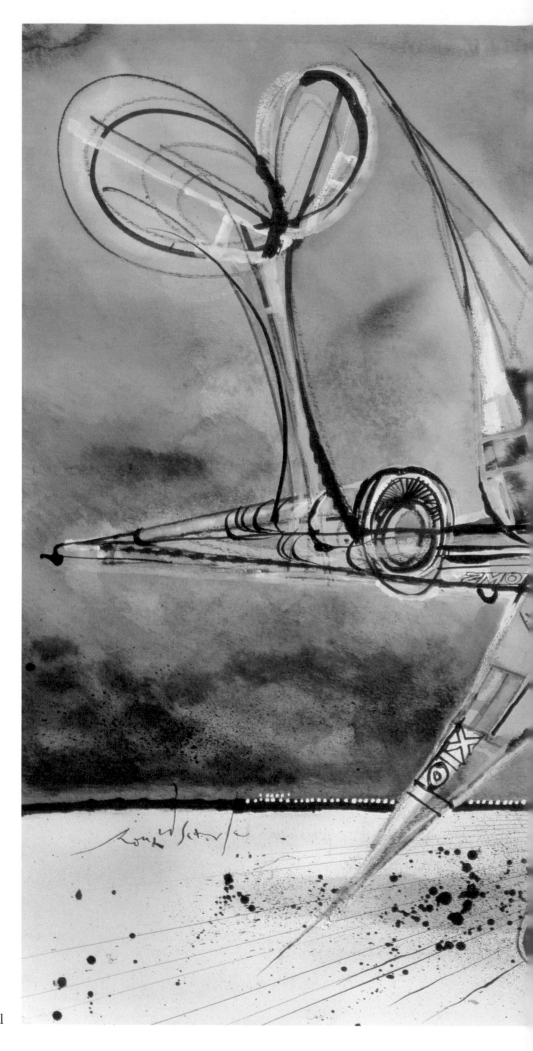

The Fool

Big Star

Strolling Players

Probably Allegorical

An angel passed… [1983]

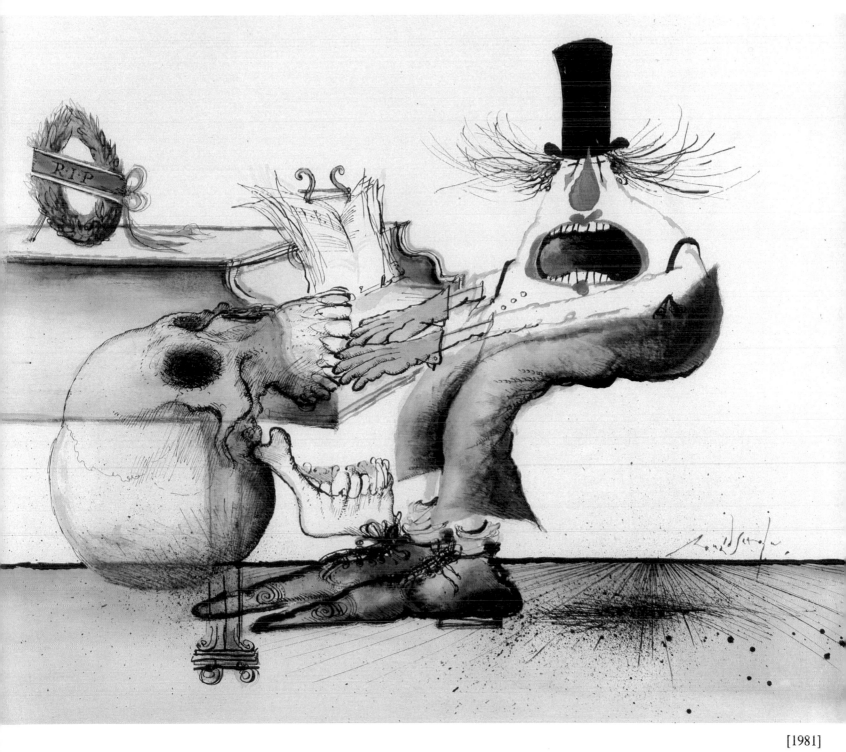

For Some Songs by Tom Lehrer

Poisoning Pigeons in the Park

The Irish Ballad

I Got It From Agnes [Not published]

National Brotherhood Week

We Will All Go Together When We Go

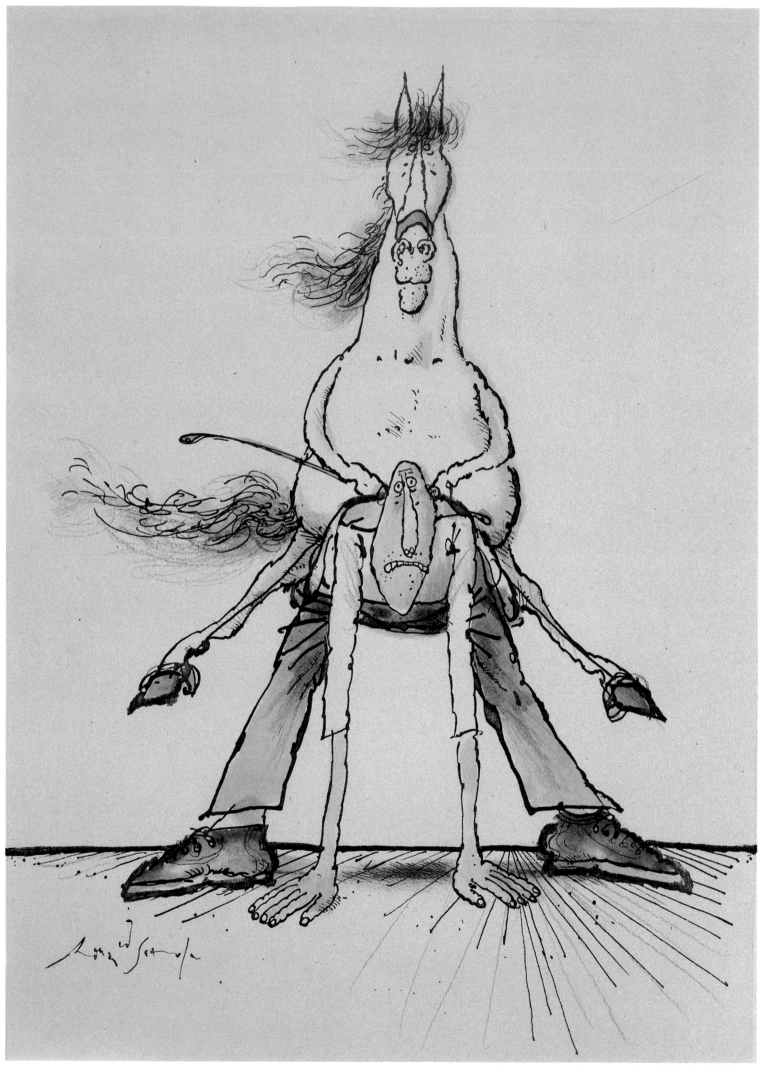

The Exchange [1981]

Some corner of a foreign field that is for ever England…

[Telescopic photo, taken through the window of the
ladies' room of a well-known Port Said hostelry.]

Above The De Hooghe medal [detail]

SOME RECENT COMMEMORATIVE MEDALS

created for the French Mint and struck
under the direction of Pierre Dehaye

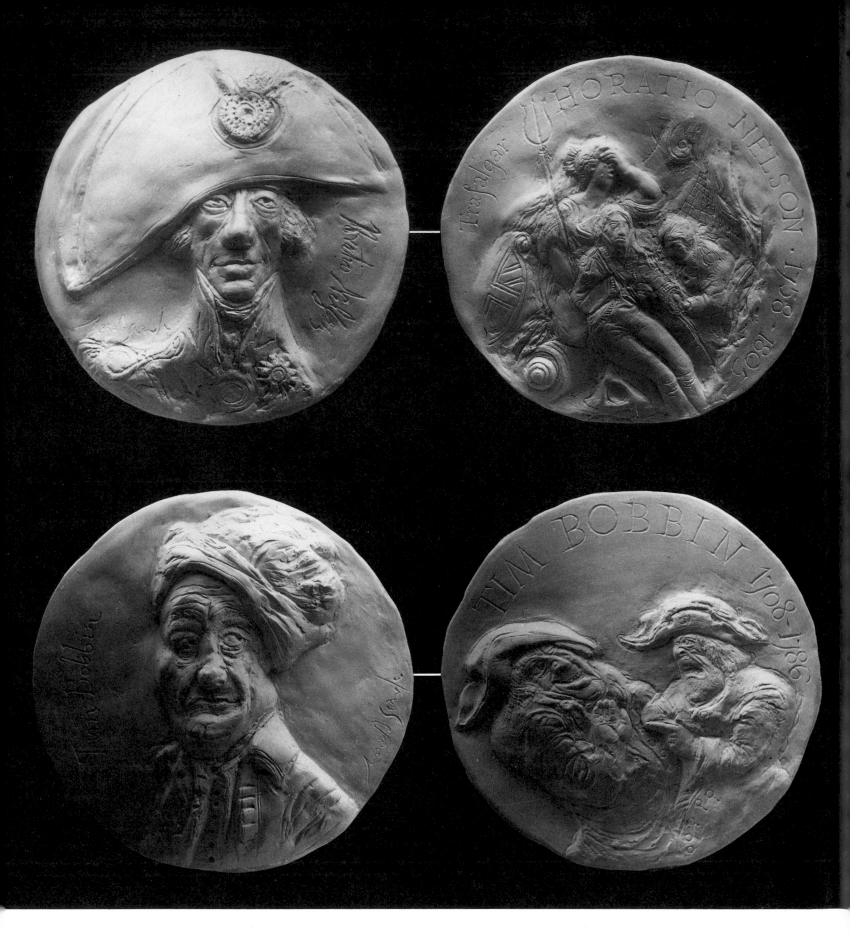

LORD NELSON   1758-1805

A commemorative medal generously struck by the French administration in honour of Nelson and Trafalgar. On the reverse, the death of Nelson – with sobbing Britannia. Based on a contemporary print by James Gillray, published shortly after the event.

'TIM BOBBIN' [John Collier]   1708-1786

Celebrating a pioneer and virtually forgotten, English caricaturist, lexicographer and humorous writer. On the reverse, two typical 'Tim Bobbin' characters, from his album, *Human Passions Delineated*, 1773.

ROMEYN DE HOOGHE   1645-1708

Medal in honour of the Dutch illustrator, satirist and one of the earliest precursors of political caricature. Reverse design based on a caricature by De Hooghe, ridiculing French adulation of the decrepit Roi Soleil, showing Louis XIV tottering in the delapidated chariot of Phoebus.

CAPTAIN FRANCIS GROSE   1731-1791

Commemorating a notable English antiquarian, amateur caricaturist and author of the first manual on the art of caricature, *Rules for Drawing Caricaturas*, published in London, 1788 and, shortly after, in France and Germany.

215

When i was young

Each time my Auntie Beat (the sister of my father) left her house,
she would firmly lock the front door & tuck the key under the doormat
outside. She would then hang a small card onto the doorknob, which
read: 'Key under mat!'

At the time this did not seem illogical to either Auntie Beat or to her relatives
and throughout my childhood i never questioned it, any more than i questioned
the fact that whatever i saw from earliest memory it was simultaneously

In the beginning, to draw was simply to note down what was already
Curious, but it did not occur to me that this was either unusual or abnormal
any more than the action of drawing, which I accepted as instinctively
as eating. Admittedly, my efforts to draw were as crude as my table-manners
were unmentionable. However, as i was soon trained to deal with both problems

like Auntie Beat with her key I remained blissfully unaware that I was born
with a defect. The abnormal was for me 'the normal'. In addition I was
born left-handed, ('Cack-handed' in local dialect) which made me an outsider in a right-handed world

give an occasional insight into many years of

a non-stop journey along a never-ending line

of uncorrected left-handed abnormality that
Caricature manifested itself in an obsession with (graphic satire & drawing)
are who are a few drawings made during a non-stop journey
along a never-ending line

NB: Must not forget to note down idea
for a flying machine & Ask Morris to
find me a fairly big bird to dissect —
& where can I find cooking of
feathers?

2 butter
milk
5× Voltarens (rouge)
buy Zwieback
Harricot ?
bring in more wood
phone Valerios
Felix
Wildski Rosenkrantz

LIST OF ILLUSTRATIONS

[*Left*] Page of the
original manuscript

20　Christmas Dinner, 1944. Changi Gaol, 10th to 25th December, 1944. Pencil on buff paper, 33 x 21cm. POW drawing No.144 Repro. *The Naked Island*, 1952

21　Kensington Bus Stop, Winter 1947. 1947. Pen and sepia ink, 22.5 x 17.5cm.

22　At the theatre: *The Stalls*. 1946. Pen and sepia ink, 25 x 20cm.

23　At the theatre: '*So sorry...*' 1946. Pen and sepia ink, 25 x 20cm.

24　Railway worker, Vranduk Yugoslavia. 22nd August 1947, Pencil.

25　Peasants, Zagreb. 6th September 1947, Pen. Col. Charles Cundall, London.

25　Old Man, Zenica, Yugoslavia. 23rd August 1947. Pen.

25　Boy, Brod, Yugoslavia. 1947. Pen and sepia ink, 20 x 16cm.

26　The Ruins of Warsaw. 11th August 1948. Pen and watercolour.

26　Polish Girl. 1948, Pen and sepia ink, 25 x 17.5cm

26　Praying Woman, Burgher's Cathedral, Krakow. 15th August 1948. Pen.

27　Beggar, at the door of Burgher's Cathedral, Krakow. 15th August 1948. Pen.

28　Street Scene, W.8 1947. Pen and gouache.

28　St. Trinian's: *How to shrink a human head*. c.1950. Pen. First published in *Lilliput* magazine, London. Repro. *Back to the Slaughterhouse*, London, 1951.

29　St. Trinian's: "*Some little girl didn't hear me say 'unarmed combat'.*" 1951. Pen and wash, 32.5 x 22cm. First published in *Lilliput*, April 1952. Repr. *Souls in Torment*, London, 1952. Coll. Victoria and Albert Museum, London.

30　St. Trinian's: "*I didn't realise it took so long.*" c.1953. Pen and sepia ink, 39 x 27.5cm. Repro. *The St. Trinian's Story*, London, 1959

31　St. Trinian's: "*Go on, say it – 'I promise to leave my body to Science'.*" c.1950. Pen and wash. First published in *Lilliput*, January 1951. Repro. *Back to the Slaughterhouse*, London 1951

31　St. Trinian's: "*I'll just die and then you'll be sorry.*" c.1953. Pen and sepia wash, 36.5 x 24cm. Repro *The St. Trinian's Story*, London 1959

31　St. Trinians: (*Girl with Lilies*). c.1953. Pen. Repro. *Souls in Torment*, London 1953.

32　St. Trinian's: "*Bloody sportsdays...*" c.1952. Pen and wash. First published in *Lilliput*, May 1952. Repro. *Souls in Torment*, London 1953

33　On the Bayswater Road. 1950. Ink and sepia wash on buff paper, 46 x 29cm.

34　Street Musician, Portobello Road. 1951. Pen and sepia wash, 30 x 23cm.

35　Street Musicians, Portobello road, 1951. Pen and sepia wash, 30.5 x 25.5cm.

36　New York: *The Bowery*. June 1957. Pen, 37 x 25.5cm. Repro. *Which Way Did He Go?* London, 1961.

37　New York: *The old Savoy Dance Hall, Harlem*. June 1957. Pen, 26 x 37cm. First published in *Punch*, 17th July 1957. Repro. *Which Way Did He Go?* London 1961

37　New York: *Cocktail Time*. June 1957. Pen. First published in *Punch*, 24th July 1957. Repro. Which Way Did He Go? London 1961

38　New York: *Broadway*. May 1957. Pen. First published in *Punch*, 24th July 1957. Repro. *Which Way Did He Go?* London 1961.

39　Refugees 1959: *Camp Laschenskyhof, near Salzburg*. 7th November 1959. Pen, sepia ink and crayon, 39 x 56cm. Repro. *Refugees*, London 1960.

39　Refugees 1959: *New Arrival, San Sabba Transit Camp, Trieste*. 11th November 1959. Pencil. Repro. *Refugees*, London 1960.

40　Refugees 1959: *Food Queue, Aversa Refugee Camp, near Naples*. 14th November 1959. Pen and sepia ink, 38 x 54.5cm. Repro. *Refugees*, London 1960.

40　Refugees 1959: *Aversa Refugee Camp, near Naples*. Refugees selling their rations to the local population. 14th November 1959. Pen and sepia ink. Repro. *Refugees*, London 1960.

41　Refugees 1959: *New Arrivals in Police Quarantine, San Sabba Camp, Trieste*. 11th November 1959. Pen and sepia ink, 38 x 52cm. Repro. *Refugees*, London 1960.

41　Refugees 1959: *Single Men's Dormitory, Camp Karls Kaserne, Vienna*. 4th November 1959. Pen and sepia ink, 39 x 53cm. Repro. *Refugees*, London 1960.

42　"*Of course, you're lucky – yours curls naturally.*" 1956. Pen and sepia wash, 36 x 43.5cm. *Punch*, 2nd January 1957.

43　Majesty of the Law. 1959. Pen and wash, 46.5 x 36.5cm. For *Holiday Magazine*, USA, August 1960. Repro. *Which Way Did He Go?* London 1960. Coll. Mr. & Mrs. Theo Larsson, Sutton.

44-45　House of Commons, 1955: *Churchill's last speech, 24th March 1955*. 1955. Pen and wash. For *Life Magazine*, New York, 4th April 1955.

45　(Man with three arms). 1957. Pen and wash drawing for *Punch*, 8th May 1957. Repro. *Which Way Did He Go?* London 1961.

46　Paris 1958: *Assemblée-Nationale-De-Gaulle*. 1958. Pen and sepia wash, 39.5 x 56cm. For *Punch*, 19th November 1958. Repro. *Which Way Did He Go?* London 1961.

46　(Poodle). c. 1960. Pen and crayon. Repro. *Which Way Did He Go?* London 1961.

47　Watch out for next week's thrilling instalment... 1968. Pen and watercolour, 27 x 20.5cm. Repro. *Hello – Where Did All the People Go?* London 1969.

48　(Girl feeding caged snail). 1968. Pen and wash. Repro. *Hello – Where Did All the People Go?* London 1969.

48　(Snail with zipper). 1968. Repro. *The Square Egg*, London 1968.

48　(Punctured snail). 1968. Pen. Repro. *The Square Egg*, London 1968.

48　(Snail rowing). 1968. Pen. Repro. *Hello – Where Did All the People Go?* London 1969.

48 (Snail bird). 1968. Pen and wash. Repro. *Hello – Where Did All the People Go?* London 1969.

49 (Foot in it). 1968. Pen. Repro. *Hello – Where Did All the People Go?* London 1969.

49 (Weeping-eye snail). 1968. Pen. Repro. *Hello – Where Did All the People Go?* London 1969.

49 (On the track). 1968. Pen. Repro. *The Square Egg*, London 1968.

49 (Bicycle snail). 1968. Pen and wash. Repro. *Hello – Where Did All the People Go?* London 1969.

50 Nixonites. 1960. Pen and sepia wash. For *Life Magazine*, New York, 31st October 1960.

50 Kennedy. 1960. Pen and sepia wash. For *Life Magazine*, New York 31st October 1960.

51 On the Road With Kennedy: *Presidential Election Campaign 1960. Kennedy v Nixon.* October 1960. Pen and sepia wash, 40 x 50.5cm. For *Life Magazine*, New York. 31st October 1960.

52-53 Adolf Eichmann on trial, Jerusalem 1961. Pen sketches made at the trial.

54 Ukraine: *Secret Soviet Missile Base.* 19659. Pen and pencil, 35.5 x 47cm. For *Punch*, 19th August 1959. Repro. *Russia For Beginners*, London 1960. Bib.Nat.Catalogue No. 183, 1973

55 Take One Toad: *Remedy for Death and Suchlike Afflictions of Some Severity.* 1968. Pen and wash. For *Take One Toad*, London 1968

56 Take One Toad: *For the Remedy of the Toothache.* 1968. Pen and wash. For *Take One Toad*, London 1968

56 Take One Toad: *For the Remedy of the Toothache.* 1968. Pen and wash. For *Take One Toad*, London 1968

57 Take One Toad: *For the Remedy of the Toothache.* 1968. Pen and wash. For *Take One Toad*, London 1968

57 Take One Toad: *For the Treatment of Ulcers, Cancers, Tumours...* 1968. Pen and wash. For *Take One Toad*, London 1968.

58 Take One Toad: *For the Treatment of Malignant Sore Throat.* 1968. Pen and wash. For *Take One Toad*, London 1968

59 Sweet Dreams. 1968. Pen. 17 x 14cm. Repro. *The Square Egg*, London 1968 Bibl.Nat.Cat.No. 141, 1973

60 Gourmet. 1966. Pen and wash, 45 x 35cm. For *The New Yorker* Magazine, 7th January 1967. Repro. *The Square Egg*, London 1968. Private coll. Frankfurt a/M.

61 The Second Coming of Toulouse-Lautrec: *Bosom Friends.* 1969. Lithograph, 26 x 24cm. Repro. *Hommage à Toulouse-Lautrec*, Paris 1969. (Plate: I, Limited Edition.) Gurlitt Cat. No. 53, 1971. Bib.Nat.Cat.No. 23, 1973. Printed by Michel Cassé, Paris.

62-63 The Second Coming of Toulouse-Lautrec: *The Labours of Hercules.* 1969. Lithograph, 50 x 65cm. Repro. *Hommage à Toulouse-Lautrec*, Paris 1969. Gurlitt Cat.No.62, 1971. Bib.Nat.Cat.No.31, 1973. Printed by Michel Cassé, Paris.

64 The Second Coming of Toulouse-Lautrec: Sketch for *Samson Demolishing the Temple*, 1969. Pen. 20.5 x 13.5cm. Repro. *Hommage à Toulouse-Lautrec*, Paris 1969.

65 Those Magnificent Men in Their Flying Machines: (a) *Birds on the Wing* (b) *Birds of Feather* 1964. Pen and watercolour, 50 x 65cm. Two of a number of drawings made for the 20th Century Fox film. Also repro. in the book of the same name, London 1965.

66 CAMBRIDGE 1964: *"Granta" Reveals All.* Cover for the Cambridge University student magazine. 1964. Pen and watercolour, 51 x 37.5cm. Coll. Wilhelm-Busch Museum, Hannover.

67 LONDON 1961: *"Are you sure this is Chris Barber's place?"* 1961. Pen, watercolour and collage (Du Maurier), 31.5 x 27.5cm. For *Punch*, 19th July 1961

68 EAST BERLIN 1964: *Frankfurter Allee (Oops), Stalinallee (Oops), Karl-Marx Allee (Oof!).* 1964. Pen and wash. Repro. *Haven't We Met Before Somewhere?* London 1966.

69 Black Forest. 1963. Pen and watercolour, 50 x 38cm. For *Holiday Magazine*, USA October 1964. Repro. *Haven't We Met Before Somewhere?* London 1966. Bib.Nat.Cat. 203, 1973. Coll. Monica Searle.

70-71 Palm Springs, California. 1963. Pen and watercolour. For *Holiday Magazine*, USA, February 1965.

72 Baseball, Phoenix Arizona. 1963. Pen and watercolour, 51 x 38cm. For *Sports Illustrated*, New York, March 1964. Bib.Nat.Cat.No. 170, 1973

73 Hudson's Bay Post, Maliotenam, Canada. 1963. Pen and watercolour, 49 x 36cm. For *Holiday Magazine*, USA April 1964. Repro. *From Frozen North To Filthy Lucre*, New York 1964 Coll. Hudson's Bay Company, Toronto.

74 Casablanca: *Family Group.* 1965. Pen and watercolour, For *Holiday Magazine*, USA September 1966.

75 HAWAII: *Hotel Street, Honolulu.* 1965. Pen and watercolour, 54 x 36cm. For *Holiday Magazine*, USA December 1965. Bibl.Nat.Cat.No.166, 1973; Berlin Cat.No.1, 1976. Coll. Dr. Hermann Warnakoff, Berleburg.

76-77 HAWAII: *Sunset Oahu.* 1965. Pen and watercolour, 36 x 54cm. For *Holiday Magazine*, USA December 1965. Bibl.Nat.Cat.No. 165, 1973. Coll. Galerie Bartsch und Chariau, Munich.

78-80 Pages from a Hamburg Sketchbook. 1967. Pen, page size 21 x 13.5cm. Repro. *Filles de Hambourg*, Paris 1969 and *Die Mädchen von Montmartre und St. Pauli*, Reinbek 1980.

81 Papa Doc', Haiti. 1968. Pen, wash and watercolour. For *Status Magazine*, New York November 1968. (Original stolen, New York 1968.)

82 The Wall, Berlin. 1963. Pen and watercolour, 50 x 38cm. Repro. *Haven't We Met Before Somewhere?* London 1966.

83. The Square Egg.
1979. Pen and watercolour, 29.5 x 23cm.
Cover drawing for the paperback version of *The Square Egg*, London 1980.

84 The Good Old Days: 1. 1972.
Coloured lithograph, 50 x 65cm.
Printed by Michel Cassé, Paris.

85 The Outsider.
1977. Pen and watercolour, 50 x 65cm.
Coll. Dr. Hermann Warnakoff, Berleburg.

86 Moment of Reflection. 1972.
Pen and watercolour, 38 x 29cm.
Coll. Mr. & Mrs. Asmus Boysen, Hamburg.

87 Notes for a déjeuner sur l'herbe.
1976. Pen, watercolour and crayon, 37 x 27cm.

88-89 Déjeuner sur l'herbe. 1976.
B&w lithograph proof, watercolour and crayon, 50 x 65cm.

90 Pigs.
1974. Pen and watercolour, 38 x 32cm.
Back cover of *Le Fou Parle*, Paris, January 1979.

91 People.
1978. Pen, 37.5 x 29.5cm.
Op.Ed.Page *New York Times*, 18th September 1979.

92-93 Horsepower.
1979. B&w lithograph proof, watercolour and crayon, 50 x 65cm.

94 Pegasus Returns.
1972. B&w lithograph proof and watercolour, 65 x 50cm.

95 Atlas.
1979. B&w lithograph proof, watercolour and crayon, 50 x 65cm.

96 Rendezvous.
1976. Pen and watercoour, 33.5 x 28.5cm.

97 Emergence of MS-tique USA (1973) with a nod to Hogarth's *Rake's Progress* (1733).
1973. Seven drawings in pen and wash, all 15.5 x 27.5cm.
DEBUT: *Bursts upon the social scene in a madcap whirl of men and money*

98 SUCCESS: *Popular with college classmates, pursues studies in natural history*

99 DISILLUSIONMENT: *Marries conglomerateur, bewails subsidiary status*

100 TEMPTATION: *Becomes radical feminist, storms male bastions*

101 DEGRADATION: *Emerges as national spokesperson for the movement*

102 DOWNFALL: *Testifies before Senate committee on Subversive Sexuality*

103 RUIN: *Appointed to U.S. Cabinet, first of her gender to become Secretary of Defense.*
Slightly modified version of the saga published in *Town & Country* Magazine, New York, August 1973.

104 Atlas Squared.
1979. Pen, 35 x 24cm.
Marathon World Magazine, USA, July 1979.

105 Secretary to the Big Boys.
1974. Pen, 40.5 x 38cm.

106 The Bureaucrat.
1974. Pen, 40.5 x 38cm. Berlin Cat.No.79, 1976.

107 Technocrat.
1974. Pen, 40.5 x 38cm.
For Voko Büromöbel, Polheim.

108 Hire and Fire.
1974. Pen, 40.5 x 38cm.
For Voko Büromöbel, Polheim.

109 Workaholic.
1974. Pen, 40.5 x 38cm.
For Voko Büromöbel, Polheim.

110 Upper Reaches.
1974. Pen, 40.5 x 38cm.
For Voko Büromöbel, Polheim.
Berlin Cat.No.77, 1976.

111 Spokesperson.
1974. Pen, 40.5 x 38cm.
For Voko Büromöbel, Polheim.

112 The Manger.
1974. Pen, 40.5 x 38cm.
For Voko Büromöbel, Polheim.
Berlin Cat.No. 78, 1976.

113 MONEY: *The Speculator.*
1973. Pen and watercolour, 50 x 32.5cm.
For *Money Magazine*, New York, February 1973.

114 MONEY: *Means nothing to me.*
1978. Pen and watercolour, 42.5 x 39cm. For *Town & Country* Magazine, New York.

115 MONEY: *Hello! Big Timer.*
1972. Pen and watercolour, 40 x 29cm.

116-117 Racin'
1979. Pen, watercolour and crayon, 32.5 x 50cm.

118-119 Huntin' (The Kill).
1978. Pen, watercolour and crayon, 50 x 65cm.

120 Swingin'
1974. Coloured lithograph, 50 x 65cm.
Printed by Michel Cassé, Paris.

121 Thinkin'
1979. Pen, 36 x 22cm.
For *Marathon World* Magazine, USA, July 1979.

122 Spring
1972. Pen, watercolour and crayon, 38 x 28cm.

123-128 SOME SIGNS OF THE ZODIAC.

123 The Signs.
1977. Pen and watercolour, 50 x 65cm.
Titlepage for the book: *Searle's Zoodiac*, London, 1977.

124 Leo
1977. Pen and watercolour, 50 x 65cm.

125 Scorpio.
1977. Pen and watercolour, 50 x 65cm.

125 Libra.
1977. Pen and watercolour, 25 x 32.5cm.

126 Virgo.
1977. Pen and watercolour, 25 x 32.5cm.
Coll. Monica Searle

127 Aries.
1977. Pen and watercolour, 50 x 65cm.

127 Gemini.
1977. Pen and watercolour, 25 x 32.5cm.

128 The Embrace.
1979. Pen and watercolour.

128 Aries.
1977. Pen and watercolour, 25 x 32.5cm.

129 Pastorale.
1975. Coloured lithograph, 50 x 65cm.
Printed by Michel Cassé, Paris.

130 Mickey Monument.
1971. Coloured etching, 76 x 57cm.

131 Haven't We Met Before Somewhere? (Unpublished book-jacket design).
1972. Pen and watercolour, 38 x 32.5cm.

132-133 They Don't Make Them Like That Anymore.
1978. Pen, watercolour and crayon, 36 x 45cm.
For *Town & Country* Magazine New York, October 1978.

134 The Kojak Connection.
1975. Pen and watercolour, 23 x 31cm.
For *T.V. Guide*, USA, 3rd January 1976.

135 The Pickled Gudgeon
Connection.
1971. Pen, crayon and collage. For
Travel & Leisure Magazine, New
York, Autumn 1971.
(Original stolen New York.)

136 God Bless You, Merry
Gentlemen...
1972. Pen and watercolour,
38.5 x 28cm.
Poster for the Royal Choral
Society, London.
Bibl.Nat.Cat.No. 252, 1973;
Berlin Cat.No. 53, 1976.
Coll. Gerhard Fischer, Munich.

137 For the Good of the People
1977. Pen and watercolour
45.5 x 24cm.

138-139 The Monster.
1978. Pen, watercolour and
crayon, 50 x 65cm.

140 Death and the Child.
1979. Three pen sketches for
UNICEF Year of the Child.

141 Suffer Little Children...
1979. Pen, watercolour and collage
45 x 34cm.
For UNICEF Year of the Child.

142 Playing Scales.
1970. Pen, 32 x 21cm.
(Original stolen USA, 1970.)

143 The Last Customer.
1973. Pen, watercolour and
crayon, 40.5 x 29cm.
Cover for *The New Yorker*
Magazine, 13th March 1973.

144 Sorceress.
1978. Pen, watercolour and
collage, 46 x 32.5cm.
Coll. Andreas Bartsch, Munich.

145 You Give Me Wings.
1980. Pen and crayon,
21 x 30cm.

146 Boxed Cat: (3)
1983. Pen, watercolour and
crayon, 26.5 x 18.5cm.

147 Boxed Cat: (2)
1983. Pen, watercolour and
crayon, 26.5 x 18.5cm.

148-159 SOME MISLAID
MASTERPIECES.

148 Study for the Mislaid
Masterpiece: *Swinger*, by
Fragonard.
1980. Pencil and crayon,
30 x 21cm.

149 Study for the Mislaid
Masterpiece: *The Raft of the
"Méduse"*, by Henri de Toulouse-
Lautrec.
1980. Pen, watercolour and
crayon, 30.5 x 34.5cm.
Coll. Vicco von Bülow,
Ammerland.

150-151 MISLAID
MASTERPIECES: *Mona's Sister,
Gladys*, by Leonardo Da Vinci
(1452-1519). 1980. Pen,
watercolour and crayon 25 x 18cm.

152-153 MISLAID
MASTERPIECES: *The Peaceable
Kingdom*, by Edward Hicks (1790-
1849). The first version, c.1829.
1974. Pen and watercolour,
50 x 65cm.
Coll. Prof. K. Sontheimer,
Munich.

154-155 MISLAID
MASTERPIECES:
Swinger, by Jean-Honoré
Fragonard (1732-1806) 1980. B&w
lithograph proof, watercolour and
crayon,
65 x 50cm

156-157 MISLAID
MASTERPIECES: *The Raft of the
"Méduse"*, by Henri de Toulouse-
Lautrec (1864-1901).
1980. Pen, watercolour and
crayon, 50 x 65cm.

158-159 MISLAID
MASTERPIECES: *Swine Lake
(Later known as Pig Lake), a ballet.*
1980. B&w lithograph proof,
watercolour and crayon, 50 x
65cm.

160 MISLAID
MASTERPIECES: *Les Très
Pauvres Heures du Duc de Berry*
(detail), École Française,
XVᵉ siécle. 1975-80. Coloured
black and white print, 20.5 x
19cm.

161 MISLAID
MASTERPIECES: *Self-Portrait as
a Non-Stop Self-Mutilator*, by
Vincent van Gogh (1853-1890).
1980. Pen, watercolour and
crayon, 35 x 26.5cm.

162-163 MISLAID
MASTERPIECES: *Bonjour
Monsieur Courbet* by Gustave
Courbet (1819-1877). The first
draft, c. 1853. 1982. Xerox,
watercolour and crayon, 21 x
30cm.

164 Back to Square One.
1982. Lithograph in 8 colours,
87 x 60.5cm.
Printed by Michel Cassé, Paris.
Unlimited lithographed 'poster' for
the Galerie Carmen Cassé, Paris.

165-170 THE SITUATION IS
HOPELESS...

165 Bar-flies.
1980. Pen, watercolour and
crayon, 29.5 x 34cm.

166 *Out-of-touch unicorn unaware
that it is a myth.*
1979. Pen, watercolour and
crayon, 32.5 x 34cm.
Private coll. London.

167 *American bald eagle suddenly
realising that its leanings are
basically Marxist.*
1979. Pen, watercolour and
crayon, 32.5 x 34cm.
Coll. Andreas Bartsch, Munich.

168 *Pathologically mixed-up
vampire but trying to conceal the fact
that its tastes are rigidly vegetarian.*
1979. Pen, watercolour and
crayon, 31.5 x 34cm.

169 *Under-sexed double-horned
rhinoceros in search of a reliable
aphrodisiac.*
1979. Pen, watercolour and
crayon, 31 x 34cm.
Coll. Dieter Burckhardt, Basle.

170 *Conceited egg about to
commence its memoirs.*
1979. Pen, watercolour and
crayon, 31.5 x 34cm.
Coll. Monica Searle.

All for the book: *The King of
Beasts*, London 1980, (later, *The
Situation is Hopeless*, 1982).

171 Look, no animals. (An
exercise.)
1978-80. Pen and crayon,
32 x 24cm.

172 How to Open a Bottle of
Wine.
1982. Pen and crayon, 30 x 21cm.
One of a series of drawings for a
booklet, *How to Open a Bottle of
Wine*. Designed for John Goelet
and the vineyards: *Clos du Val*,
California and *Taltarni*, Australia.

173-178 SOME GREAT WINE
CEREMONIES.
Part of a series of drawings
designed for the *Clos du Val* Wine
Co. Ltd., Napa Valley, California
and *Taltarni* wines, Moonambel,
Australia.

173 *Annual Reunion of the
Confrérie of Cork Sniffers.* 1981.
Pen, watercolour and crayon,
45 x 32.5cm.
Coll. Mr. & Mrs. John Goelet,
New York.

174 *The Annual Non-Arrival of
the English Grape Ceremony.* 1980.
Pen, watercolour and crayon,
45 x 32.5cm.
Coll. Mr. & Mrs. John Goelet,
New York.

175 *AUSTRALIA: Uncorking the Kangarouge.*
1980. Pen, watercolour and crayon, 45 x 32.5cm.
Coll. Mr. & Mrs. John Goelet, New York.

176 *GERMANY: The Ancient, Noble (and Secret) Ceremony of Slashing the Trockenbeerenauslese.*
1981. Pen, watercolour and crayon, 45 x 32.5cm.
Coll. Mr. & Mrs. John Goelet, New York.

177 *FRANCE: The Annual Festival of Welcome to Italian Wines.*
1981. Pen, watercolour and crayon, 45 x 32.5cm.
Coll. Mr. & Mrs. John Goelet, New York.

178 *The Japanese Wine Ceremony.*
1980. Pen, watercolour and crayon, 45 x 32.5cm.
Coll. Mr. & Mrs. John Goelet, New York.

179 *God Yama and a Dead Soul.*
Publicity illustration for Suntory Old (Japanese) Whisky.
1981. Pen, 32.5 x 26.5cm.
Mainichi Shimbun, Tokyo 6th September 1981.
Coll. Takeshi Kaiko, Tokyo.

180-181 The Encounter.
1981. Pen and watercolour, 65 x 50cm.
Repro. *Big Fat Cat Book*, London, 1982.

182 Confused Albatross shooting an Ancient Mariner.
1982. Pen, watercolour and crayon, 43 x 33cm.
For *Animal Kingdom* magazine, New York.

183-200 STRICTLY FOR THE BIRDS.

183 *"You'll never get me up in one of those things."*
1974 and 1982. Pen, watercolour and crayon, 20.5 x 13cm.

184-185 *Crusade.*
1980. Pen, watercolour and crayon, 50 x 65cm.

186-187 *Warm Engines.*
1980. Pen, watercolour and crayon, 50 x 65cm.

188-189 *Wake.*
1980. Pen, watercolour and crayon, 55 x 75cm.

190-191 *Irresistible force meets immovable object.*
1980. Pen, watercolour and crayon, 50 x 65cm.

192-193 *The Fool.*
1980. Pen, watercolour and crayon, 50 x 65cm.
Coll. Monica Searle.

194-195 *Big Star.*
1980. Pen, watercolour and crayon, 50 x 65cm.

196-197 *Strolling Players.*
(Suffering from jet lag).
1980. Pen, watercolour and crayon, 50 x 65cm.

198-199 *Probably Allegorical.*
1980. Pen, watercolour and crayon, 50 x 65cm.
Coll. Bank für Gemeinwirtschaft, Frankfurt a/M.

200 "*Quo Vadis?*"
1981. Pen sketch, 14.5 x 20cm.

201 *Strictly for the Birds.*
1981. Pen, watercolour, crayon and collage, 65 x 50cm.

202 An angel passed…
1983. Lithography, watercolour and crayon, 29 x 23cm.

203-208 FOR SOME SONGS BY TOM LEHRER.

203 *Album cover design.*
1980. Pen and watercolour, 45 x 39cm.
Coll. Monica Searle.

204 *Poisoning Pigeons in the Park.*
All the world seems in tune
On a spring afternoon,
When we're poisoning pigeons
   in the park.
Ev'ry Sunday you'll see
My sweetheart and me,
As we poison the pigeons
   in the park.
1980. Pen, 32.5 x 45cm.

205 *The Irish Ballad.*
About a maid I'll sing a song,
   Sing rickety-tickety-tin,
About a maid I'll sing a song
Who didn't have her family long.
Not only did she do them wrong,
   She did ev'ryone of them in,
                  them in,
   She did ev'ryone of them in.
1980. Pen, 32.5 x 45cm.

206 *I got it from Agnes.*
(Dropped by the publishers)
1980. Pen, 32.5 x 45cm.

207 *National Brotherhood Week.*
....
It's National Ev'ryone-smile-at-
one-another-hood Week,
Be nice to people who
Are inferior to you.
It's only for a week, so
   have no fear,
Be grateful that it doesn't
   last all year.
1980. Pen, 32.5 x 45cm.

208 *We Will All Go Together When We Go.*
....
And we will all bake together
   when we bake,
There'll be nobody present at
   the wake.
With complete participation
In that grand incineration,
Nearly three billion hunks of
   well-done steak.
1980. Pen, 32.5 x 45cm.

Quotations from *Too Many Songs by Tom Lehrer*, Copyright © 1981 by Tom Lehrer. Simultaneously published by Eyre Methuen, London, Pantheon Book, New York and Random House of Canada Ltd., Toronto, 1981. *All rights reserved.*

209 Boxed Cat: (1)
1983. Pen, watercolour and crayon, 26.5 x 18.5cm.

210 Roughshod Rider.
1983. Pen and watercolour, 27 x 19cm.

211 The Exchange.
1981. Pen, watercolour and crayon, 65 x 50cm.
Repro. *The Big Fat Cat Book*, London 1982.

212 Some corner of a foreign field that is for ever England…
Telescopic photo, taken through the window of the ladies' room of a well-known Port Said hostelry.
1981. Pen and crayon, 21.5 x 21cm.
Coll. Monica Searle.

213 Some recent commemorative medals created for the French Mint and struck under the direction of Pierre Dehaye.

Enlarged detail of the medal to Romeyn De Hooghe.

214 Lord Nelson 1758-1805.
Medal struck in bronze and silver, June 1981. Limited edition of 100 examples, diam. 76mm. General edition, diam. 68mm.

214 'Tim Bobbin' (John Collier) 1708-1786.
Medal struck in bronze, June 1980.
Limited edition of 100 examples, diam. 76mm. General edition, diam. 68mm.

215 Romeyn De Hooghe (1645-1708).
Medal struck in bronze, February 1981. Limited edition of 100 examples, diam, 76mm. General edition, diam. 68mm.

215 Captain Francis Grose
(1731-1791).
Medal struck in bronze, October
1980. Limited edition of 100
examples, diam. 76mm. General
edition, diam. 68mm.

216 Page of the original
manuscript.
1978. Pen, ink, watercolour,
crayon, tea, coffee, côte du Rhone,
etc., etc. 30 x 19cm.

217 The Old Dope Peddler.
Tailpiece for the album, *Too Many
Songs by Tom Lehrer*, London,
New York and Toronto 1981.
(See 203-208.)
1980. Pen, crayon and collage,
12 x 13cm.

BOOKS BY RONALD SEARLE

Forty Drawings, Cambridge 1946
Le nouveau ballet anglais, Paris 1946
Hurrah for St. Trinian's, London 1948
The Female Approach, London 1949
Back to the Slaughterhouse, London 1951
Souls in Torment, London 1953
The Rake's Progress, London 1955
Merry England, Etc., London 1956
Which Way Did He Go? London 1961
From Frozen North to Filthy Lucre, New York 1964
Searle in the 'Sixties, London 1964
Pardong M'sieur, Paris 1965
Searle's Cats, London 1967
The Square Egg, London 1968
Hello – Where Did All the People Go? London 1969
Filles de Hambourg, Paris 1969
Hommage à Toulouse-Lautrec, Paris 1969
The Addict, London 1971
More Cats, London 1975
Drawings from Gilbert & Sullivan, London 1975
Searle's Zodiac, London 1977
Ronald Searle (Monograph), Reinbek bei Hamburg 1978
Die Mädchen von Montmartre und St. Pauli, Reinbek bei Hamburg 1980
The King of Beasts & Other Creatures, London 1980
Ronald Searle's Big Fat Cat Book, London 1982
The Illustrated Winespeak, London 1983

ANTHOLOGIES

Weil Noch das Lämpchen glüht, Zürich 1952
Médisances, Paris 1953
The Female Approach, New York 1954
The Penguin Ronald Searle, London 1960
I desegni di Ronald Searle, Milan 1973
Von Katzen und anderen Menschen, Berlin (DDR) 1981

IN COLLABORATION

Paris Sketchbook (with Kaye Webb), London 1950
The Terror of St. Trinian's (with D.B. Wyndham-Lewis), London 1952
Down With Skool (with Geoffrey Willans), London 1953
Looking at London (with Kaye Webb), London 1953
How To Be Topp (with Geoffrey Willans), London 1954
Whizz for Atomms (with Geoffrey Willans), London 1956
The Compleet Molesworth (with Geoffrey Willans), London 1958
The Dog's Ear Book (with Geoffrey Willans), London 1958
The Big City (with Alex Atkinson), London 1958
Back in the Jug Agane (with Geoffrey Willans), London 1959
The St. Trinian's Story (with Kaye Webb), London 1959
U.S.A. for Beginners (with Alex Atkinson), London 1959
Refugees 1960 (with Kaye Webb), London 1960
Russia for Beginners (with Alex Atkinson), London 1960
Escape from the Amazon! (with Alex Atkinson), London 1964
Those Magnificent Men in Their Flying Machines (with B. Richardson
and A. Andrews), London 1965
Haven't We Met Before Somewhere? (with Heinz Huber), London 1966
Monte-Carlo or Bust! (with J. Davies, K. Annakin and A. Andrews),
London 1969
The Great Fur Opera (with Kildare Dobbs), Toronto 1970
Paris! Paris! (with Irwin Shaw), New York 1977

ACKNOWLEDGEMENTS

The Publishers wish to thank the following persons for their assistance in bringing together the material for this book: Tessa Sayle of the Tessa Sayle Literary & Dramatic Agency, London; John Locke and Nonnie Locke of John Locke Studios, New York; Andreas Bartsch of the Bartsch & Chariau Gallery, Munich; Michel Cassé, lithographer and Carmen Cassé of the Galerie Carmen Cassé, Paris; John Goelet, New York for drawings originally designed to promote his vineyards *Clos du Val*, California and *Taltarni*, Australia; and Monica Searle for editing in three languages.

Colour and black and white photography by Rosmarie Nohr, Munich; Graham Bush, London; Vidachrome, New York; André Chadefaux and Claudia Desclozeaux, Paris.